THE TRUTH ABOUT MONEY

MEYER BENDAVID

REVISION ONE

Contents

Acknowledgement

I would like to thank my lovely wife and avid golf partner, Cecile, for her love, encouragement and support; my talented son and daughter, Michael and Susan, for making me so proud to be their father; my wonderful daughter in-law Diana; and my extraordinary grandchildren, Shani, Leeza and Adam, for being such a source of delight.

Copyright 2011

About the Author

In 1987 I established myself as a licensed, <u>full-service broker</u> working with Dean Witter, Financial West Group, and National Planning Corporation. I specialized in mutual funds, stocks, bonds, annuities, life and health insurance. As a <u>money manager,</u> I was responsible for assisting my clients with purchasing securities that conformed to their risk level and helping them meet their financial goals toward retirement.

In 2003 I retired as a stock broker and decided to consolidate my business and work as an independent insurance agent. I have been assigned to the largest service company in the United States selling life insurance. I recently published the books "The Easy Way to Tax-free Savings," "The Money Tracking Machine," and "Craps." These books are sold worldwide.

Meyer Bendavid
<u>meyer5757@aol.com</u>   Web site –
http://www.thekeystosuccess.com

Chapter 1 - Money and the Common Good

Money – Money – Money

When we look at almost everything that we do, it concerns money. This book will try to explain in the simplest terms the money problems we have today and find some solutions. The truth about money ideas will help you or your business succeed.

For a better understanding of problems we face today- it is necessary to get a brief understand of macroeconomics and microeconomics and the relationship to your personal finance.

What will be discussed are the national problems and solutions used in the past and solutions that could be used in the future. Even from the beginning of the United States, the founding fathers understood money problems created by the banking industry. Benjamin Franklin, Thomas Jefferson, Abraham Lincoln, J.F. Kennedy and others understood the problems plaguing society over the years, and how adjustments were made for the betterment of society.

Today countries around the world have the worst monetary problems and the largest unemployment since the great depression of the 1930's. You will be presented with ideas to make you more aware of what is happening now- and propose some solutions for the monetary and budget systems used today.

A Brief Understanding

From the Encyclopedia Britannica-
Macroeconomics is the study of national or regional economies in terms of the total amount of goods and services produced, the total income earned, the level of employment of productive resources, and the general behavior of the price of goods purchased. Until the 1930s most economic analysis concentrated on individual firms and industries. Growth in the field of macroeconomics paralleled the development of the concepts of national income and production statistics. Further macroeconomic study was spurred by attempts to understand the underlying causes of the Great Depression. The policy goals that macroeconomists typically associate with the discipline include economic growth, price stability, and full employment.

From the Encyclopedia Britannica-
Microeconomics is the study of the economic behavior of individual consumers, firms, and industries and the distribution of total production and income among them. It considers individuals both as suppliers of labor and capital and as the ultimate consumers of the final product, and it analyzes firms both as suppliers of products and as consumers of labor and capital. Microeconomics seeks to analyze the market or other type of mechanism that establishes relative prices among goods and services and allocates society's resources among their many alternative uses.

Changes are required to fix the economy and providing critical thinking to help you and the country to succeed. Even our founding fathers had problems and tried to make changes for the benefit of everyone.

From the Merriam-Webster dictionary-

The term common good: of or relating to a community at large: public <work for the *common* good>
Or: known to the community <*common* nuisances>
Or: belonging to or shared by two or more individuals or things or by all members of a group <a *common* friend>

Defining the Common Good

There are two different societies that are constantly at odds with each other. One is the *We Society* working more for the common good, and the other is the Me society that is more self-centered in their thinking caring less about you. This book will deal with the *We Society* working more for the common good.

Our founding fathers incorporated the ideas of running this country from England and Europe whose societies were run by monarchs. The structure of the monetary system and budgets first established, have never been updated to relate to our current society.

The prime example of failures in our society and other societies is due to the greed of the banking industry and the inadequate budget systems still used today. There were many who tried to make adequate changes to help society and never quite succeeded to the fullest extent. We will start off with our countries founding fathers ideas to change society and continue until present with new changes and ideas that could create a better society.

Chapter 2- Reports and the Presidential Letters

Reports Regarding Money

The following is a report about Benjamin Franklin. Benjamin Franklin's drive for self-improvement tied into a desire to improve the world around him as well. As a young tradesman in Philadelphia, Franklin's ambition, mixed with his intellectual energy and sociable nature, made him a natural leader of public projects.

In 1727, Franklin gathered eleven friends to form the (*) Junta, a club that met weekly to discuss ways of working together for the benefit of themselves and the Philadelphia community. Over several years of activity- Franklin and his associates enriched community life in Philadelphia- helping establish vital institutions and by carrying out various civic initiatives.

Franklin called his mission for improving the lives of ordinary citizens furthering the "common good." He was a true philanthropist who believed that the challenges of society must be met with mutual enterprise, cooperation, and generosity.

Even with his many personal accomplishments, Franklin's commitment to the common good was a lifelong endeavor. This activity first prompts everyone to think of things they can do to further the common good and then conveys their ideas in the form of objectives. You should:

• Understand that Franklin highly valued the power of people working together and believed good deeds could be accomplished best through alliances

• Learn that, in addition to his familiar roles as a scientist and statesman, Franklin also was a community leader whose initiatives left a lasting mark on Philadelphia and on American Society.

(*)In 1727, Benjamin Franklin convinced 12 of his friends to form a club dedicated to mutual improvement. Meeting one night a week, these young men discussed the topics of the day. The group lasted for 40 years and eventually became the nucleus of the American Philosophical Society.

Junta, pronounced who-n-toe, was a private forum for discussion and as a surreptitious instrument for leading public opinion. One of the functions of the group was to brainstorm publicly beneficial ideas.

Franklin described the Junta this way in his autobiography. I should have mentioned before, that, in the autumn of the preceding year, [1727] I had formed most of my ingenious acquaintance into a club of mutual improvement, which we called the JUNTO; we met on Friday evenings.

The rules that I drew up required that every member, in his turn, should produce one or more queries on any point of Morals, Politics, or Natural Philosophy [physics], to be discussed by the company; and once in three months produce and read an essay of his own writing, on any subject he pleased.

Our debates were to be under the direction of a president and to be conducted in the sincere spirit of inquiry after truth, without fondness for dispute or desire of victory; and to prevent warmth, all expressions of positive opinions, or direct contradiction, were after some time made contraband, and prohibited under small pecuniary penalties.

The results of the original Junta are still evident today as an integral part of American Society. The Junta gave us our first library, volunteer fire departments, the first public hospital, police departments, paved streets and the University of Pennsylvania. They recommended books, shopkeepers, and friends to each other. They fostered self-improvement through discussions on topics related to philosophy, morals, economics, and politics.

It is these accomplishments and ideals that inspired this web page. The managers of Junta Society are from across the nation. It was ordinary citizens who came together through various internet political discussion groups, for the purpose of the betterment of American Society and politics. We seek to accomplish this by providing our visitors with easy access to

information on current events and historical works which
have shaped our nation.

Presidential Letters

*Thomas Jefferson and others insisted that money creation belongs in government not private banks. Banking institutions, paper money, and paper speculation are capable of undermining the nation's stability and could be a danger in time of war. The Constitution does not empower the Congress to establish a National Bank. Rather than trust the nation's currency to private hands, the circulating medium should be restored to the nation itself to whom it belongs.

Quotes by Thomas Jefferson on the Money Policy From the web site http://www.rapidtrends.com/quotes-by-thomas-jefferson-on-monetary-policy/

The Founders understood the importance of honest money and tried to protect our money from the bankers. A review of this nation's economic history reveals that bankers, in concert with traitors in Congress, gained control of the money system, set up private "national" banks, and began implementing its mechanisms of usury and were then taken down.

Two times Andrew Jackson, our 7th president (1829-1837) brought the nation to within about $32,000 of solvency after decommissioning "The Second Bank of the United States (1818-1836)" and restoring Congressional control of our money.

It took the bankers 70 years to buy their way back into Congress to control the creation and issuance of Americans' money. The Federal Reserve was commissioned in 1913 through a series of corrupt manipulations by key members of Congress in cahoots with the Robber Barons.

Since that time, the purchasing power of the dollar has been in steady decline. Making matters even worse, the Federal Reserve Bank's monetary policy has obliterated 94 per cent of the value of the U.S. dollar. A basket of goods and services that cost $100.00 in 1913 now costs $1,673.00.

The hard assets of the nation have been in transition to the bankers and the governments are increasingly indebted to the unelected, international cabal of private bankers Congress commissioned to manage the U.S. money system.

Members of Congress, past and present, either know that one of its important functions is to protect Americans' money from the international bankers or they are not qualified to represent our interests in government. That means, at this fundamental level, every sitting member of Congress is either a traitor or an ignoramus. We know of only one exception.

Thomas Jefferson on coin and paper currency:

Speak as [gold and silver coin] as a National Resource. "In such a nation [as ours], there is one and one only resource for loans, sufficient to carry them through the expense of a war; and that will always be sufficient, and in the power of an honest government, punctual in the preservation of its faith. The fund I mean is the mass of circulating coin. Everyone knows that although not literally, it is nearly true, that every paper dollar emitted banishes a silver one from the circulation. A nation, therefore, making its purchases and payments with bills fitted for circulation, thrusts an equal sum of coin out of circulation. This is equivalent to borrowing that sum, and yet the vendor receiving payment in a medium as effectual as coin for his purchases or payments, has no claim to interest. And so the nation may continue to issue its bills as far as its wants require, and the limits of the circulation will admit…, the only resource which the government could command with certainty, the States have unfortunately fooled away, nay corruptly alienated to swindlers and shavers, under the cover of private banks." ~Letter to John W. Eppes, 1813

(John W. Eppes. [Son-in-law, Chairman of the Committee of Ways and Means of the House of Representatives]Poplar Forest, September 11, 1813.)

The Dangers of Paper Money- "That paper money has some advantages is admitted. But that its abuses also are inevitable and, by breaking up the measure of value, makes a lottery of all private property, cannot be denied." ~Letter to Josephus B. Stuart, 1817

"All the capital employed in paper speculation is barren and useless, producing, like that on a gaming table, no accession to itself, and is withdrawn from commerce and agriculture where it would have produced addition to the common mass… It nourishes in our citizens habits of vice and idleness instead of industry and morality… It has furnished effectual means of corrupting such a portion of the legislature as turns the balance

between the honest voters whichever way it is directed."
~Letter to George Washington, 1792

"I sincerely believe... that banking establishments are more dangerous than standing armies, and that the principle of spending money to be paid by posterity under the name of funding is but swindling futurity on a large scale." ~Letter to John Taylor, 1816

"[The] Bank of the United States... is one of the most deadly hostility existing, against the principles and form of our Constitution... An institution like this, penetrating by its branches every part of the Union, acting by command and in phalanx, may, in a critical moment, upset the government. I deem no government safe which is under the vassalage of any self-constituted authorities, or any other authority than that of the nation, or its regular functionaries." ~Letter to Albert Gallatin, 1803

In meeting the Banking Problem--"The monopoly of a single bank is certainly an evil. The multiplication of them was intended to cure it; but it multiplied an influence of the same character with the first, and completed the supplanting the precious metals by a paper circulation. Between such parties the less we meddle the better." ~Letter to Albert Gallatin, 1802.

Chapter 3- Monetary Plans

The Lincoln Monetary Plan

The Struggle-*From:*
http://thatsjustbob.com/politicalblog/2765/revive-lincolns-monetary-policy-an-open-letter-to-president-obama/

The bankers had Lincoln's government over a barrel, just as Wall Street has Congress in its vice-like grip today.

The North needed money to fund a war, and the bankers were willing to lend it only under circumstances that amounted to extortion, involving staggering interest rates of 24 to 36 percent. Lincoln saw that this would bankrupt the North and asked a trusted colleague to research the matter and find a solution.

In what may be the best piece of advice ever given to a sitting President, Colonel Dick Taylor of Illinois reported back that the Union had the power under the Constitution to solve its financing problem *by printing its money as any sovereign government?* Taylor said:

"Just get Congress to pass a bill authorizing the printing of full legal tender treasury notes...and pay your soldiers with them and go ahead and win your war with them also. If you make them full legal tender...they will have the full sanction of the government and be just as good as any money; as Congress is given that express right by the Constitution."

The Greenbacks actually were just as good as the bankers' banknotes. Both were created on a printing press, but the banknotes had the veneer of legitimacy because they were "backed" by gold. The catch was that this backing was based on "fractional reserves," meaning the bankers held only a small fraction of the gold necessary to support all the loans represented by their banknotes.

The "fractional reserve" ruse is still used today to create the impression that bankers are lending something other than mere debt created with accounting entries on their books. Lincoln took Col. Taylor's advice and funded the war by printing paper notes backed by the credit of the government. These legal-tender U.S. Notes or "Greenbacks" represented receipts for labor and goods delivered to the United States.

They were paid to soldiers and suppliers and were tradable for goods and services of a value equivalent to their service to the community. The Greenbacks aided the Union not only in winning the war but in funding a period of unprecedented economic expansion.

Lincoln's government created the greatest industrial giant the world had yet seen. The steel industry was launched, a continental railroad system was created, a new era of farm machinery and cheap tools was promoted, free higher education was established, government support was provided to all branches of science, the Bureau of Mines was organized, and labor productivity was increased by 50 to 75 percent.

The Greenback was not the only currency used to fund these achievements; but they could not have been accomplished without it, and they could not have been accomplished on money borrowed at the usurious rates the bankers were attempting to extort from the North.

Lincoln succeeded in restoring the government's power to issue the national currency, but his revolutionary monetary policy was opposed by powerful forces. The threat to established interests was captured in an editorial of unknown authorship, said to have been published in The London Times in 1865:

"If that mischievous financial policy which had its origin in the North American Republic during the late war in that country, should be used down to a fixture, then that-

Government will furnish its own money without cost. It will pay off its debts and be without debt. It will become prosperous beyond precedent in the history of the civilized governments of the world. The brains and wealth of all countries will go to North America. That government must be destroyed or it will destroy every monarchy on the globe."

Lincoln was assassinated in 1865. According to historian W. Cleon Souse:

"Right after the Civil War there was considerable talk about reviving Lincoln's brief experiment with the Constitutional monetary system. *Had not the European money-trust intervened, it would have no doubt become an established institution.*"

The institution that became established instead was the Federal Reserve, a privately-owned central bank given the power in 1913 to print Federal Reserve Notes (or dollar bills) and lend them to the government.

The government was submerged in a debt that has grown exponentially since, until it is now not able to be multiple trillion dollars. Following Success- Lincoln did not invent government-issued paper money. Rather, he restored a brilliant innovation of the American colonists.

According to Benjamin Franklin, it was the colonists' home-grown paper "scrip" that was responsible for the remarkable abundance in the colonies at a time when England was suffering from the ravages of the Industrial Revolution.

Like with Lincoln's Greenbacks, this prosperity posed a threat to the control of the British Crown and the emerging network of private British banks, prompting

The King to ban the colonists' paper money and require the payment of taxes in gold.

According to Franklin and several other historians of the period, it was these onerous demands by the Crown, and the corresponding collapse of the colonists' paper money supply, that actually sparked the Revolutionary War.

Abraham Lincoln's Monetary Policy, of 1865 Page 91 of Senate Document 23

Money is the creature of law and the creation of the original issue of money should be maintained as the exclusive monopoly of national Government. Money possesses no value to the State other than that given to it by circulation.

Capital has its proper place and is entitled to every protection. The wages of men should be recognized in the structure of and in the social order as more important than the wages of money.

No duty is more imperative for the Government than the duty it owes the people to furnish them with a sound and uniform currency, and of regulating the circulation of the medium of exchange so that labor will be protected from a vicious currency, and commerce will be facilitated by cheap and safe exchanges.

The available supply of Gold and Silver being wholly inadequate to permit the issuance of coins of intrinsic value or paper currency convertible into coin in the volume required to serve the needs of the People, some other basis for the issue of currency must be developed, and some means other than that of convertibility into coin must be developed to prevent undue fluctuation in the value of paper currency or any other substitute for money of intrinsic value that may come into use.

The monetary needs of increasing numbers of people advancing towards higher standards of living can and should be met by the Government. Such needs can be served by the issue of National Currency and Credit through the operation of a National Banking system. The circulation of a medium of exchange issued and backed by the Government can be properly regulated and redundancy of issue avoided by withdrawing from circulation such amounts as may be necessary by Taxation, Redeposit, and otherwise. Government has the power to regulate the currency and credit of the Nation.

Government should stand behind its currency and credit and the Bank deposits of the Nation. No individual should suffer a loss of money through depreciation or inflated currency or Bank bankruptcy.

Government possessing the power to create and issue currency and credit as money and enjoying the right to withdraw both currency and credit from circulation by Taxation and otherwise need not and should not borrow capital at interest as a means of financing Governmental work and public enterprise.

The Government should create, issue, and circulate all the currency and credit needed to satisfy the spending power of the Government and the buying power of the consumers.

The privilege of creating and issuing money is not only the supreme prerogative of Government, but it is the Governments greatest creative opportunity. By the adoption of these principles the long felt want for a uniform medium will be satisfied.

The taxpayers will be saved immense sums of interest, discounts, and exchanges. The financing of all public enterprise, the maintenance of stable Government and ordered progress, and the conduct of the Treasury will become matters of practical administration.

The people can and will be furnished with a currency as safe as their own Government. Money will cease to be master and become the servant of humanity.

A Complete Reversal

The colonists won the war but ultimately lost the money power to a private banking cartel, one that issued another form of paper money called "banknotes." Today the bankers' debt-based money has come to dominate most of the economies of the world; but there are a number of historical examples of the successful funding of economic development in other countries simply with government-issued credit.

In Australia and New Zealand in the 1930s, the Depression conditions suffered elsewhere were avoided by drawing on a national credit card issued by publicly-owned central banks. The governments of the island states of Guernsey and Jersey created thriving economies that carried no federal debt, just by issuing their own debt-free public currencies. China has also funded impressive internal development through a system of state-owned banks. Here in the United States, the state of North Dakota has a wholly state-owned bank that creates credit on its books just as private banks do.

This credit is used to serve the needs of the community, and the interest on loans is returned to the government. Not coincidentally, North Dakota has a .2 billion budget surplus at a time when 46 of 50 states are insolvent, an impressive achievement for a state of isolated farmers battling challenging weather. The North Dakota prototype could be copied not only in every U.S. state but at the federal level.

The JF Kennedy Monetary Plan

From: *http://www.john-f-
kennedy.net/executiveorder11110.htm*

President John Kennedy,
The Federal Reserve
and Executive Order 11110
by Cedric X
from the Final Call, Vol. 15, No.6, On Jan. 17, 1996

On June 4, 1963, a little known attempt was made to strip the Federal Reserve Bank of its power to loan money to the government at interest.

On that day President John F. Kennedy signed Executive Order No. 11110 that returned to the U.S. government the power to issue currency, without going through the Federal Reserve. Mr. Kennedy's order gave the Treasury the power "to issue silver certificates against any silver bullion, silver, or standard silver dollars in the Treasury."

This meant that for every ounce of silver in the U.S. Treasury's vault, the government could introduce new money into circulation. In all, Kennedy brought nearly $4.3 billion in U.S. notes into circulation. The ramifications of this bill are enormous. With the stroke of a pen, Mr. Kennedy was on his way to putting the Federal Reserve Bank of New York out of business.

If enough of these silver certificates were to come into circulation they would have eliminated the demand for Federal Reserve Notes. This is because the silver certificates are backed by silver and the Federal Reserve Notes are not backed by anything.

Executive Order 11110 could have prevented the national debt from reaching its current level, because it would have given the government the ability to repay its debt without going to the Federal Reserve and being charged interest in order to create the new money

Executive Order 11110 gave the U.S. the ability to create its own money backed by silver.

After Mr. Kennedy was assassinated just five months later, no more silver certificates were issued. The Final Call has learned that the Executive Order was never repealed by any U.S. President through an Executive Order and is still valid.

Why then has no president utilized it? Virtually all of the nearly $6 trillion in debt has been created since 1963, and if a U.S. president had utilized Executive Order 11110 the debt would be nowhere near the current level.

Perhaps the assassination of JFK was a warning to future presidents who would think to eliminate the U.S. debt by eliminating the Federal Reserve's control over the creation of money. Mr. Kennedy challenged the government of money by challenging the two most successful vehicles that have ever been used to drive up debt - war and the creation of money by a privately-owned central bank.

His efforts to have all troops out of Vietnam by 1965 and Executive Order 11110 would have severely cut into the profits and control of the New York banking establishment.

As America's debt reaches unbearable levels and a conflict emerges in Bosnia that will further increase America's debt, one is forced to ask, will President Clinton have the courage to consider utilizing Executive Order 11110 and, if so, is he willing to pay the ultimate price for doing so?

Kennedy's Executive Order

Executive Order 11110 Amendment of Executive Order No. 10289

As Amended, Relating to the Performance of Certain Functions Affecting the Department of The Treasury By virtue of the authority vested in me by section 301 of title 3 of the United States Code, it is ordered as follows:

Section 1. Executive Order No. 10289 of September 19, 1951, as amended, is hereby further amended- By adding at the end of paragraph 1 thereof the following subparagraph (j):

(j) The authority vested in the President by paragraph (b) of section 43 of the Act of May 12, 1933, as amended (31 U.S.C.821(b)), to issue silver certificates against any silver bullion, silver, or standard silver dollars in the Treasury not then held for redemption of any outstanding silver certificates, to prescribe the denomination of such silver certificates, and to coin standard silver dollars and subsidiary silver currency for their redemption and – By revoking subparagraphs (b) and (c) of paragraph 2 thereof.

Sec. 2. The amendments made by this Order shall not affect any act done, or any right accruing or accrued or any suit or proceeding had or commenced in any civil or criminal cause prior to the date of this Order but all such liabilities shall continue and may be enforced as if said amendments had not been made.

John F. Kennedy The White House, June 4, 1963. Of course, the fact that both JFK and Lincoln met the same end is a mere coincidence.

The Christian Law Fellowship

There has been exhaustively researched Kennedy's ordeal through the Federal Register and Library of Congress. We can now safely conclude that this Executive Order has never been repealed, amended, or superseded by any subsequent Executive Order. In simple terms, it is still valid.

From: *http://politicalvelcraft.org/2011/04/19/jfk-killed-just-days-after-shutting-down-rothschilds-fed-reserve-in-1963-secret-memo-shows-president-signed-executive-orders-eo-11-and-eo-110/*

JFK Killed Just Days after Shutting down Rothschild's Fed Reserve In 1963: Secret Memo Shows President Signed Executive Orders EO-11 and EO-110 that are STILL IN FORCE BUT NOT ENFORCED.

Rothschild gained by burying the TRUTH behind the Executive Orders 11,110 that protected the U.S. Citizens by shutting down the High Taxation process in Paying Interest to ROTHSCHILD'S Fed Reserve Printing Machine.

Remember how psychotic the reasoning was behind The Vietnam War and how Johnson/Nixon prevented The U.S. from winning that war? The Vietnam War started in 1954 & JFK scheduled the ending of that war by 1965, but Johnson/Nixon kept it going

Until January 15, 1973. Well who gained from 8 more years of a financed war and with many years to come in interest payments for the money borrowed on the war effort from Rothschild?

The United States suffered 58,119 killed, 153,303 wounded, not too bad in the depopulation arena either for the ole British Monarchy. The U.S. Citizen is to own their own money, not Rothschild.

President John F. Kennedy exterminated the Rothschild Federal Reserve System, as did President Lincoln Who Was Also Assassinated for the same. In 1963, JFK signed Executive Orders EO-11 and EO-110, returning to the government the constitutional responsibility to print money, taking that privilege away from the Rothschild International Federal Reserve System where it was absconded in 1913.

On June 4, 1963, a virtually unknown Presidential decree, Executive Order 11110, was signed with the authority to basically strip the Rothschild Bank of its power to loan money to the United States Federal Government at interest. With the stroke of a pen, President Kennedy declared that the privately owned Rothschild Federal Reserve Bank would soon be out of business.

Executive Order 11110 should have prevented the national debt from reaching its current level (virtually all of the nearly $11 trillion in federal debt has been created since 1963) if LBJ or any subsequent President were to enforce it. It would have almost immediately given the U.S. Government the ability to repay its debt without going to the private Federal Reserve Banks and being charged interest to create new "money". Executive Order 11,110 gave the U.S.A. the ability to; once again, create its own money backed by silver and realm value worth something.

Chapter 4 – The Federal Reserve

Democracy Rises-Up Superior to the Money Power

The Federal Reserve - a Private Corporation One of the most common concerns among people who engage in any effort to reduce their taxes is, "will keeping my money hurt the government's ability to pay its bills?"

As explained in the first article in this series, the modern withholding tax does not, and wasn't designed to, pay for government services. What it does do, is pay for the privately-owned Federal Reserve System.

Black's Law Dictionary defines the "Federal Reserve System" as, "Network of twelve central banks to which most national banks belong and to which state chartered banks may belong. Membership rules require investment of stock and minimum reserves."

Privately-owned banks own the stock of the Fed. This was explained in more detail in the case of Lewis v. United States, Federal Reporter, 2nd Series, Vol. 680, Pages 1239, 1241 (1982), where the court said:

Each Federal Reserve Bank is a separate corporation owned by commercial banks in its region. The stock-holding commercial banks elect two thirds of each Bank's nine member board of directors. Similarly, the Federal Reserve Banks, though heavily regulated, are locally controlled by their member banks. Taking another look at Black's Law Dictionary, we find that these privately owned banks actually issue money:

Federal Reserve Act Law which created Federal Reserve banks which act as agents in maintaining money reserves, issuing money in the form of bank notes, lending money to banks, and supervising banks Administered by Federal Reserve Board (q.v.).

The FED banks, which are privately owned, actually issue, that is, create the money we use. In 1964 the House Committee on Banking and Currency, Subcommittee on Domestic Finance, at the second session of the 88th Congress, put out a study entitled Money Facts which contains a good description of what the FED is:

The Federal Reserve is a total money-making machine. It can issue money or checks. And it never has a problem of making its checks good because it can obtain the $5 and $10 bills necessary to cover its check simply by *asking the Treasury Department's Bureau of Engraving to print them.*

As we all know, anyone who has a lot of money has a lot of power. Now imagine a group of people who have the power to create money. Imagine the power these people would have. This is what the Fed is. No man did more to expose the power of the Fed than Louis T.

McFadden, who was the Chairman of the House Banking Committee back in the 1930s. He constantly pointed out that monetary issues shouldn't be partisan by criticizing the Herbert Hoover and Franklin Roosevelt administrations. In describing the Fed, he remarked in the Congressional Record, House pages 1295 and 1296 on June 10, 1932, that: Mr. Chairman, *we have in this country one of the most corrupt institutions the world has ever known.* I refer to the Federal Reserve Board and the Federal Reserve banks.

The Federal Reserve Board, a Government Board, has cheated the Government of the United States and the people of the United States out of enough money to pay the national debt. The depredations and the iniquities of the Federal Reserve Board *and the Federal reserve banks acting together have cost this country enough money to pay the national debt several times over.*

This evil institution has impoverished and ruined the people of the United States; has bankrupted itself, and has practically bankrupted our Government. It has done this through the maladministration of that law by which the Federal Reserve Board, and through the corrupt practices of the moneyed vultures who control it. Some people think the Federal Reserve banks are United States Government institutions.

They are not Government Institutions

They are private credit monopolies which prey upon the people of the United States for the benefit of themselves and their foreign customers; foreign and domestic speculators and swindlers; and rich and predatory money lenders. In that dark crew of financial pirates there are those who would cut a man's throat to get a dollar out of his pocket; there are those who send money into States to buy votes to control our legislation;

And there are those who maintain an international propaganda for the purpose of deceiving us and of wheedling us into the granting of new concessions which will permit them to cover up their past misdeeds and set again in motion their gigantic train of crime.

Those 12 private credit monopolies were deceitfully and disloyally foisted upon this country by bankers who came here from Europe and who repaid us for our hospitality by undermining our American institutions.

The Fed basically works like this: The government granted its power to create money to the Fed banks. They create money, and loan it back to the government charging interest. The government levies income taxes to pay the interest on the debt. On this point, it's interesting to note that the Federal Reserve act and the sixteenth amendment, which gave congress the power to collect income taxes, were both passed in 1913. The incredible power of the Fed over the economy is universally admitted. Some people, especially in the banking and academic communities, even support it.

On the other hand, there are those, both in the past and in the present that speak out against it. One of these men was President John F. Kennedy. His efforts were detailed in Jim Marrs' 1990 book, Crossfire:

Another overlooked aspect of Kennedy's attempt to reform American society involves money. Kennedy apparently reasoned that by returning to the constitution, which states that *only Congress shall coin and regulate money*, the soaring national debt could be reduced by *not paying interest* to the bankers of the Federal Reserve System, *who print paper money then loan it to the government at interest.*

He moved in this area on June 4, 1963, by signing Executive Order 11,110 which called for the issuance of $4,292,893,815 in United States Notes through the U.S. Treasury rather than the traditional Federal Reserve System.

That same day, Kennedy signed a bill changing the backing of one and two dollar bills from silver to gold, adding strength to the weakened U.S. currency. Kennedy's comptroller of the currency, James J. Saxon, had been at odds with the powerful Federal Reserve Board for some time, encouraging broader investment, and lending powers for banks that were not part of the Federal Reserve System.

Saxon also had decided that non-Reserve banks could underwrite state and local general obligation bonds, again weakening the dominant Federal Reserve banks. A number of "Kennedy bills" were indeed issued - the author has a five dollar bill in his possession with the heading "United States Note" - but were quickly withdrawn after Kennedy's death.

According to information from the Library of the Comptroller of the Currency, Executive Order 11,110 remains in effect today, although successive administrations beginning with that of President Lyndon Johnson apparently have simply ignored it and instead returned to the practice of paying interest on Federal Reserve Notes.

Today we continue to use Federal Reserve Notes, and the deficit is at an all-time high. The point being made is that the IRS taxes you pay aren't used for government services. It won't hurt you, or the nation, to legally reduce or eliminate your tax liability.

Chapter 5 – Mark Pash

Mark Pash's Ideas on the Monetary Policy

http://cpe.us.com/article/monetary-policy/
Mark Pash CFP – Founder and Chairman

Mark Pash grew up and worked in two separate family businesses, one in manufacturing and the other in retail stores. Mark went on to receive two business degrees, a Bachelors and Masters, from UCLA and USC, respectively. Then he served, as an officer, in the business branch of the U.S. Army- the Quartermaster Corp. After the army, he received his Certified Financial Planners designation from the College of Financial Planning.

Over the past 40 years Mark has been very active in the financial industry helping clients with their budgets, investments, loans, income taxes, social security, medical coverage and scores of other person financial issues. Additionally, Mark has founded a number of financial organizations and has served as an officer of various industry corporations and associations. His extensive background brings a grounded understanding of the practical and theoretical in the field of economics. Mark has long been active in politics and was a Congressional candidate in 2002 in California's 27th Congressional District.

You will be able to find his information at
http://cpe.us.com/articles/
in the article on monetary policy.

Article 1, Section 8, Clause 5 was created for congress -to coin Money, regulate the Value thereof, and of foreign Coin, and fix the Standard of Weights and Measures. Congress gave the handling of money to the Federal Reserve, a private organization, in 1913.

This system creates new money only by issuing debt– to private institutions and to the government. Actually speaking the national debt has been around since 1835 when Andrew Jackson was president. Private debt-money is only created by the commercial banks under the regulation of the Federal Reserve.

The government *Treasury* debt-money is only created directly by the Federal Reserve's "open market" operations at the Federal Reserve bank in New York." The Federal Reserve is called a central bank. If too much money is issued, we could have inflation and if too little is issued for many needs we could have a recession or depression.

The U.S. *Treasury* issues a bond or note for the money needed and the *Federal Reserve records it as an asset* and the *Treasury records it as a debt.* The Federal Reserve issued the money with no funds of its own. It is called money from nothing, debt money or debt backed money.

The Federal Reserve deposits the issued money from the *treasury* into commercial banks like Bank of America, Chase, Wells Fargo, or Citibank. This starts the private (money) monetary creation system, which is usually much larger than the government's creation through *Treasuries*. The system allows a bank to <u>create new money on small deposits as declared by the Federal Reserve Board,</u>

The Fractional Reserve Requirement

As an example: *If the reserve requirement is 10% then the bank can loan from a deposit of $1,000 another $900 or 90% of the value of the $1000. Then this new $900 loan is deposited in another bank, which then can make another $810 loan. This process repeats itself until a maximum of $9,000 is loaned out by the commercial banks from the initial deposit of $1,000.* All the new money created was debt or "debt backed money."

The big question is: If all money is created through debt, where does the money come from to pay the interest charges by these banks? <u>Where is it written that money has to be created only from debt?</u>

Problems- If money is not spread around or circulated depressions or recessions occur. Look back starting around 1837, 1857, 1873, 1893, 1907 and the Banking Crisis of 1884 and the recessions of 1892-6, 1904 and 1921 and the depression from 1873 to 1879 and the Great Depression of the 1930's and the World War II recessions of the 50's, 80's and 90's and our current Great Recession, which began in 2007 and learn what happened.

The current problems were caused by <u>the lack of circulation and sub-prime loans collapse</u>- (issuing mortgage loans without enough down payments, or collateral necessary for the loan) which went all over the world. How did this happen and was it necessary?

At present the only way we get needed money into circulation is through the issuance of debt-loans (private & public). These *archaic* banking ideas *do not fit the needs of our economy today*. Today's private system usually lends for those that qualify when times are good, and then if problems start to occur you can only borrow if you already have money or collateral.

This lack of circulation of money started boom-or-bust scenarios, not only in specific industries but also in the entire economy, stifling growth, competition, recirculation of money and employment.

The *elimination* of the *Glass-Steagall Act has allowed almost unlimited access of the monetary creation process to the commercial banking owned investment-trading companies resulting in our current financial crises.

*From Wikipedia, the free encyclopedia-
The Glass-Steagall Act) -The Banking Act of 1933, enacted June 16, 1933, was a law that established the Federal Deposit Insurance Corporation (FDIC) in the United States and introduced banking reforms, some of which were designed to control speculation. It is most commonly known as the Glass–Steagall Act, after its legislative sponsors, Carter Glass and Henry B. Steagall.

Some provisions of the Act, such as Regulation Q, which allowed the Federal Reserve to regulate interest rates in savings accounts, were repealed by the Depository Institutions Deregulation and Monetary Control Act of 1980. Provisions that prohibit a bank holding company from owning other financial companies were repealed on November 12, 1999, by the Gramm–Leach–Bliley Act.

The repeal of provisions of the Glass-Steagall Act of 1933 by the Gramm-Leach-Bliley Act effectively removed the separation that previously existed between the Wall Street investment banks and depository banks. This repeal directly contributed to the severity of the Financial crisis of 2007–2010. Others argue that repealing the provisions had little impact on the financial system and even helped restore stability during the financial crisis.

The <u>Dodd–Frank Wall Street Reform and Consumer Protection Act</u> is a federal statute in the United States that was signed into law by President Barack Obama on July 21, 2010. The Act is a product of the financial regulatory reform agenda of the 111th United States Congress and the Obama administration.

Journalist <u>Gretchen Morgenson</u> argues that the Dodd–Frank Act is not strong enough, arguing that it fails to protect consumers adequately, and, more importantly, fails to cut big and interconnected financial entities down to size.

Think-tanks such as the <u>CEE Council</u> have argued that the dismantlement of the Glass–Steagall Act was only the symptom of a much deeper problem: the emergence of a new economic paradigm associating the worst interpretations of <u>Keynesian</u> monetary stimulus with unbridled deregulation that came to define the Clinton and Bush eras (1993–2009). In that perspective, they view the Dodd–Frank Act as insufficient, lacking the broad provisions necessary to restore financial orthodoxy and minimize conflicts of interests.

Other faults- of this system is that new money gets into the economy only using debt instruments using variable-short term interest rate charges. Besides rising debt, rising interest rates hurt the borrowers that don't have too much money and any organizations or businesses that use debt- instead of equity as a means of financing their operations.

<u>Where does the interest money come from to pay the banks?</u> There is no money created to pay the interest- only the principle of the loan. If the economic has problems and bankruptcy occurs when individuals and business struggle to find interest from each other, the interest isn't available. This is a disastrous win-lose scenario.

Why are there so many failures- People make mistakes? When a single money creation system creates an error, it puts the entire system in jeopardy and stops or reduces money into the economy causing an extreme economic down turn. This also causes a slower than necessary recovery.

Some solutions- How about a complete reform with many new money delivery systems? Considering the failures of private and central banking over centuries, *we must eliminate the private fractional reserve system of money creation from the commercial banking system and eliminate the <u>interest charges</u> on the National Debt.*

Using state banking systems helps to reduce favoritism, favoring based on kinship, bribes, or appointment of a political hanger-on without regard of their qualifications, shoddy management and criminal activity.

Reduce over lending in successful industries and individuals. It makes managing risks less difficult. By creating more business opportunities, competition is increased; money is circulated; and hardship and inequity are reduced. Businesses fail for lack of money- not competition or mismanagement. Increasing the number of businesses should provide an increase in money. Credit should be based on the ability to succeed- not just on the ability to repay- and should also be based on the quality of your talent and need for your enterprise- not just the quantity of your collateral.

Absolute power corrupts absolutely. Eliminate the monopolistic power of money or creating excess money- by reducing the power that only one system brings to creating money. Open up the capability to divert money from industries that do not need it to those who do. This will lower the causes of recession/depression. Lower the volatility due to defaults and bankruptcies. Reduce over- lending to specific individuals, companies, industries, or geographical areas are critical by offering different objectives that should control over-lending.

Offer a better way to eliminate a bubble economy by controlling money for consumer loans and the stimulation of business loans. Provide more money to areas with high need, such as low-tech industries and lower income areas.

Human error and judgment in a multiplicity of systems can be much more easily overcome resulting in less chance of a catastrophe. The fiscal system has many governments such as – federal, state, county and city with many systems such as – military, Medicare, social security, education and welfare. All money would be operated at a much more diversified level.

Improve and increase regulations and risk models. Reckless lending will be scattered. It would be easier for Congress to cope with globalization having a more stabilized monetary policy having fewer defaults and using equity rather than debt. The level of greed would be lowered. Even with checks and balances limiting error is essential for the economy. Sharing risk by developing novel ideas to offset risky private enterprises that slow economic development is critical for future generations. Human hardships will be greatly reduced.

Chapter 6- The Budget

The Current and Suggested Budget System

Everyone knows the Government's *treasury* can print money- therefore there is no debt. The ideas of using *treasury* money for necessary projects needed by states, cities and municipalities are not new. Businesses should have access to the *treasury* money doing required maintenance or new development- thereby hiring many people to do the work- stimulating the economy.

In watching C-span and the arguments that occur over problems of the budget are not necessary and distract from the real problems people face daily. Arguments occur on cuts of benefits for the common good and could be easily solved without putting hardship on everyone. Questions are being brought up about the debt limits by the government. The *static budget* systems for government, states and cities and municipalities are *extremely limited and antiquated.*

Foreign countries, corporations, companies, and individuals buy treasury bills, bonds, notes, or other debt instruments from the U.S. Government. The U.S. treasury accumulates moneys from the sales. All debt instruments purchased must be paid interest and can be bought back by a specified time.

The treasury should print money, but issues <u>debt instruments</u> to the Federal Reserve to create money. The money is used for paying the interest debt and used to stimulate the economy. The money is also used for preserving some businesses from going bankrupt and issuing refunds for almost everyone with the idea to stimulate buying and other uses. The idiotic idea of issuing debt instruments causes the debt limit to increase daily to over eleven trillion dollars.

Static budgets are fine provided sufficient moneys are received by taxes collected and allocated for *normal needs for the year.* Of course unforeseen resulting problems occur, where not enough money is collected, and the problems are larger than the budget, thereby creating debts to the cities, municipalities, territories, states, and federal government with reductions in needed programs to maintain common needs, education, etc.

What is the <u>flexible</u> budget? A flexible budget adjusts or flexes for changes in any activity. The flexible budget is more sophisticated and useful than a static budget which remains the same regardless of the volume of an activity. Flexible budgeting is not nearly as complicated as you might think. It is more of a principle of business philosophy than an accounting technique. Simply stated, it's a budget that takes into account <u>marginally</u> unpredictable events and how it might affect spending.

Without having a flexible budget you can see the problems we face today. The following is a letter from the governor of California to the people of California talking about the static budget problems facing everyone.

Open Letter to the People of California by Jerry Brown Governor of California December 5, 2011.

When I became Governor again -- 28 years after my last term ended in 1983 -- California was facing a $26.6 billion budget deficit. It was the result of years of failing to match spending with tax revenues as budget gimmicks instead of honest budgeting became the norm.

In January, I proposed a budget that combined deep cuts with a temporary extension of some existing taxes. It was a balanced approach that would have finally closed our budget gap.

I asked the legislature to enact this plan and to allow you, the people of California, to vote on it. I believed that you had the right to weigh in on this important choice: should we decently fund our schools or lower our taxes? I don't know how you would have voted, but we will never know. The Republicans refused to provide the four votes needed to put this measure on the ballot.

Forced to act alone, Democrats went ahead and enacted massive cuts and the first honest on-time budget in a decade. But without the tax extensions, it was simply not possible to eliminate the state's structural deficit.

The good news is that our financial condition is much better than a year ago. We cut the ongoing budget deficit by more than half, reduced the state's workforce by about 5500 positions and cut unnecessary expenses like cell phones and state cars. We actually cut state expenses by over $10 billion. Spending is now at levels not seen since the seventies. Our state's credit rating has moved from "negative" to "stable," laying the foundation for job creation and a stronger economic recovery.

Unfortunately, the deep cuts we made came at a huge cost. Schools have been hurt and state funding for our universities has been reduced by 25%. Support for the elderly and the disabled has fallen to where it was in 1983. Our courts suffered debilitating reductions.

The stark truth is that without new tax revenues, we will have no other choice but to make deeper and more damaging cuts to schools, universities, public safety and our courts.

That is why I am filing today an initiative with the Attorney General's office that would generate nearly $7 billion in dedicated funding to protect education and public safety. I am going directly to the voters because I don't want to get bogged down in partisan gridlock as happened this year. The stakes are too high.

My proposal is straightforward and fair. It proposes a temporary tax increase on the wealthy, a modest and temporary increase in the sales tax, and guarantees that the new revenues be spent only on education. Here are the details:

Millionaires and high-income earners will pay up to 2% higher income taxes for five years. No family making less than $500,000 a year will see their income taxes rise. In fact, fewer than 2% of California taxpayers will be affected by this increase.

There will be a temporary ½ cent increase in the sales tax. Even with this temporary increase, sales taxes will still be lower than what they were less than six months ago.

This initiative dedicates funding only to education and public safety--not on other programs that we simply cannot afford.

This initiative will not solve all of our fiscal problems. But it will stop further cuts to education and public safety.

I ask you to join with me to get our state back on track.

Jerry Brown

What should be the New Common Good for a Flexible Budget?

Imagine the different departments of the US government, the states, territories, counties, cities and municipalities- not having a debt problem, and have the capability to obtain money without having to reduce necessary functions simply by borrowing from the U.S. Treasury. The U.S. treasury can print money without a debt.

This is particularly important everywhere in the United States where unpredictable events, alter the common good. *Why do we have to wait for disasters to occur before something is started? The cost for procrastination is extremely high, not only in damage or dollars, but to loss of life.*

All the new functions of the flexible budget should maintain historical data on how certain unpredictable events alter budgetary costs. This revised flexible budgeting technique is designed to overcome the many limitations involved with a static budget that does not respond to changing conditions, such as the increased need to improve the common good, and the excess needs of income to avoid suffering because of lack of money.

The recovery could be done by maintaining a high level of investing to find new ways of consuming, and to distribute money to be used to increase employment supporting the common good.

When workers have no means of keeping the economy growing because of lack of money to buy, the flexible budgeting system should be used to start increasing demand, (creating jobs) thereby increasing consumption.

With the new concept of flexible budget accounting, the treasury, states, counties, cities, municipalities, and businesses can alter their plans and decisions immediately enabling them to respond to uncertainty with lightning rapidity.

Currently most state, city, and municipal budgets are in the red. <u>Current budgeting procedures require everyone to reduce the common good to maintain a balanced budget. That is absolutely ridiculous.</u>

What are the Functions? Flexible budgeting can be used for increasing or decreasing business activity and should be used as efficiently as possible, no matter what the reason. An example to stimulate business and competition could be projects correcting floods on the Mississippi river. Prior flooded areas reached the forty two foot level near Memphis Tennessee forcing dams to be opened to relieve the stress, which resulted in flooding millions of acres near New Orleans.

How about the development of flood control canals to move water westward to areas that need water by lowering rivers that have constant floods every year? This would be considered a long term idea with jobs for millions of people around the United States.

Look around the east coast and the south and determine the amount of damage created by floods and business disruption each year. Look at the savings and now, Imagine water being moved to western areas of the U.S. that have drought conditions. There are water shortage problems in Las Vegas, Phoenix, a good section of Texas, Los Angeles, and all of southern California plus other states in the same status. *An example of projects done quite a few years ago:* Southern California obtains its water from Northern California and an aqueduct system was developed.

To start this project the *treasury* prints and uses the money specifically for the <u>bidding of contracts only for businesses located in the United States.</u> How many people could be hired to do that project? What type of jobs would that be? The list would start with Construction, trucking, electrical, jobs creating pumping stations, lumber companies, cement companies, etc. Can you imagine what could be produced by the channeling effort? How about electrical power plants, recreation areas, new towns, and cities. The states, cities and municipalities would request money from the *treasury* for such things as-

Maintenance of roads, bridges, waste water treatment, general construction, increasing electrical power grids, building housing for the poor, schools, medical research, transportation, etc. and developing plans for creating new industries, including ideas on getting rid of fossil fuel.

What are the Effects? Another major challenge in flexible budget accounting is to set realistic limits of how much the budget will change. This enables the planner to find a "mean point" for expenses that can be used as a more general guideline for budgetary expenditures to use for more long term planning. Determine the highs, lows and likely outcomes for each expense in order to maximize the return on investment for putting the time into this more complicated form of budgetary planning.

What are the benefits? All of the additional work that goes into effective flexible- budgeting does end up paying off. The organizational process would be from the *bottom upward*. Municipalities, cities, counties, states, and the *treasury* would establish working groups setting priorities from the most critical and work downward.

Banks for the common good (state banks) should be operational in every state and territory. Money will be directed to each bank used for all critical needs. Examples of *critical needs* would be tornadoes, hurricanes, volcanoes, fires, floods, earthquakes, etc. Any critical multi-state problems should be included. *Who would help if there was no FEMA?*

Critical Examples- Katrina, 911, floods across the south, wild fires in Texas, and tornadoes across Kansas, Georgia, etc. FEMA is too slow in responding. FEMA recently ran out of money to cover tornado and hurricane damage, and had to request extra money from congress. This process is too slow. Listing of companies across the U.S. should be on alert to start protecting or building immediately. The *treasury* pays everything immediately.

Example of a long term goal would be- building high speed rail systems across the U.S or in many states, fixing the road systems across the United States. I'm sure you can add more to this list.

What are the problems? At present there is plenty of money in the banks to be used by businesses to do all that is required to fix things that need fixing and are holding a lot of money in reserve and are unsure about the economy- and don't want to take chances on loaning money that may be defaulted.

What about inflation? If new money comes from the *treasury* to fix things that need fixing or used to create projects such as moving flood water westward for those states needing water, would the excess money dilute the value of the dollar?

As an example; after the First World War, Germany was in dire straits to fix the aftermath of a war.

They kept on issuing deutschmarks to be used to fix everything that needed fixing and the value of the deutschmark kept dropping. There was deutschmarks you cut with a scissor and printed 1,000,000 deutschmarks and stamped 2,000,000. The inflation factor was so high- that money wouldn't even buy a loaf of bread. The devaluation of money destroys everyone. Everyone had suffered.

Banks for the common good could be used to offset the recession we are in, by hiring businesses to do the work, employing thousands of people, and pushing forward the circulation of money to stimulation the economy. When the unemployment level drops, private banking could feel more comfortable in starting to loan money, then banks for the common good (state banks) would slowly stop the stimulation process as lending and business activity starts increasing.

Inflation is always on everyone's mind as the money starts to increase as jobs start to open up. *Inflation is caused by the lack of products or services that people desire.* One of the ways of lowering inflation is to loan money to businesses to increase the production of products to meet the demand. Another way to offset inflation is to lower everyone's spendable dollars to slow the economy. The best way to offset inflation is to increase competition. When competition increases, quality usually increases, and prices have a tendency to fall.

An example of inflation- If you wanted to buy something and there is one product and many people wanting to buy, prices could be raised continuously as long as there is a demand. An example of lowering inflation, is if you wanted to buy something and very few others want to buy and the seller has too much of the one product, those selling would have to drop prices to get rid of products.

The objection invariably rose to government-issued currency or credit is that it would create dangerous hyperinflation. However, in none of these models has that proven to be true. Price inflation results either when the supply of money goes up but the supply of goods doesn't, or when speculators devalue currencies by massive short selling, as in those cases of Latin American hyperinflation when printing-press money was used to pay off foreign debt.

When new money is used to produce new goods and services, price inflation does not result because supply and demand rise together. Prices did increase during the American Civil War, but this was attributed to the scarcity of goods common in wartime rather than to the Greenback itself.

War produces weapons rather than consumer goods. Today, with trillions of dollars being committed for bailouts and stimulus plans, another objection to Lincoln's solution is likely to be, "The government is already printing its own money – and lots of it."

This, however, is a misconception. What the government prints are bonds – its I.O.U.s or debt. If the government did print dollars, instead of borrowing them from a privately-owned central bank that prints them, Uncle Sam would not have a multi-trillion dollar millstone hanging around its neck. As Thomas Edison astutely observed:

"If our nation can issue a dollar debt instrument, it can issue a dollar bill. The element that makes a debt instrument good makes the bill good, also. The difference between the debt instrument and the bill is that the debt instrument lets money brokers collect twice the amount of the debt instrument and an additional 20%.

The currency pays nobody but those who contribute directly in some useful way. It is absurd to say that our country can issue millions in debt instruments and not millions in currencies. Both are promises to pay, but one promise fattens the usurers and the other helps the people." A change is required-

Henry Ford observed at about the same time: *"It is well enough that people of the nation do not understand our banking and monetary system, for if they did, I believe there would be a <u>revolution</u> before tomorrow morning."*

Chapter 7- Thoughts by
Meyer Bendavid

Since the Treasury can Print Money
There is no Debt

The current monetary and budget plans are not perfect and mistakes happen. New delivery systems have to be designed to reduce the mistakes or wrong decisions. The creating of money has to be placed back into a democratically elected Congress with checks and balances.

Let's look at some ideas that will convince you for the need of a new approach that <u>increases the number of systems to handle the *treasuries* money</u>. How about the *treasury* at the <u>top level</u> and <u>putting rigid requirements on the Federal Reserve</u> or *nationalizing* the Federal Reserve? Can you see <u>each state</u> and <u>territories having</u> *two banking systems* <u>getting their money directly from the *treasury*</u>?

The *first* banking system would transfer needed money directly to the commercial banking industry with the understanding; this is a debt to them and interest must be paid back to the *treasury*. The commercial banks and private banks <u>should be restricted from creating new money</u>. All checks, balances, and restrictions come directly from the state controllers, attorney generals, insurance commissioners and treasurer.

The *second* banking system would be used only for the common good. The *treasury* will issue silver certificates backed by the U.S. government. If money is needed for problems that are out of the norm such as extra water needs for Las Vegas, Phoenix, parts of Texas, California, or for tornado recovery, or hurricanes, flooding, highways, bridges, sewer systems, etc., the coordination between states and the *treasury* take effect immediately to get the projects going. Businesses do the projects and get paid directly from the states- common good- banks. If states, cities, and municipalities have budget problems, money is allocated from the common good banks. If the commercial and private banks do not give out loans, the common good banks will, thereby raising competition against the commercial and private banks.

The *second state banking system* will give money to businesses with the understanding they would be hiring people in the United States to do necessary service related work to restart money circulation. They must offer good wages and benefits and establish unions. As unemployment starts to drop, commercial and private banks should start loaning money. At that time the *second state banking system* would start withdrawing money to eliminate potential inflation.

*Fighting Back-*The usury law for disciplinary interest rates should be enacted for everyone. *(The word usury from the encyclopedia referrers to interest that was charged by deducting it from the <u>loaned</u> money itself, before the loaned money was handed over to the debtor, or referred to interest that was charged by adding it to the amount due to be repaid.)*

The law states that interest cannot exceed a certain percent and should be charged on everyone. The current disciplinary system of high interest rates punishes the weakest by charging an exorbitant rate while others pay nothing. The reducing of bank lending and over-borrowing in a particular country, or group of countries is essential with each lender paying sufficient heed to the extent of their collective total commitment.

*Restoring Regulations-*The Glass-Steagall Act has to be reinstated for- regulating interest rates in savings accounts and prohibit a bank holding company from owning other financial companies. Removing the monetary creation process from the banks and increasing the diversity of distribution provides more support for the real economy rather than the financial sector. It also increases competition and reduces inequality.

Doing Something- In order to change the way the banking system works today is going to be a fight against those that control the money. That is mainly the Federal Reserve, banks, big business, those that hate big government, and those that have been brainwashed thinking everything is OK and there is a debt, care little about you, and keep fighting against the *common good.* This includes many in congress that do not understand the concept that since *the government can print money there is no debt.*

Some Ideas for Change- I'm sure you have many ideas of your own. The monetary (money) systems and budgets need changing. Freeing up treasury money to help unemployment is the key to getting the economy functioning properly.

The next topics- deal with changes around the United States where the average citizen is starting to stand up for themselves and the rights for a secure society. This is what is happening now. Included will be some suggestions.

Chapter 8 – Changes Around the United States

Fighting Back for their Rights

The unions and teachers organizations in Wisconsin marched against the governor and the state assembly republican majority to prevent the taking away of benefits and organizational rights to meet with management, discussing wages and benefits, the dismissal of teacher's benefits, and the slashing of educational funds. Those state assembly people that voted to repeal the rights and slash benefits and funds are being sued. The governor is being recalled (this takes a year in Wisconsin.) Petitions are being signed to put the recall of the Wisconsin Governor on the ballot. In other states organizations and a lot of seniors are going against the republicans for trying to change Medicare and Medical into voucher programs.

In one republican district in New York, a democrat had never been voted into congress within the last 50 years. The public stood up against a republican that was in favor of a voucher amendment and a democrat won that district by a majority. The major problem for all of the states is lack of working people and the so called debt.

Floods have continued over the years destroying property and crops. So far nothing has been done to correct flooding. One ideas mentioned before was channeling water from flooded areas westward where water is needed.

Our schools have been hit extremely hard by this recession. Cuts have been made to educational programs and teachers have been forced to retire or cut from their jobs. The worst part is the closure of schools. Teachers in the California colleges and universities have gone on rolling strikes as a measure to the California State Universities Trustees to emphasize the need for teachers and to reduce the costs of enrollment for education. Thousands of teachers and students backed by the national AFL/CIO picketed the universities. Autos and trucks driving by highlighted their encouragement.

Action needed-The idea to maintain schools and lowing of tuition for students could be direct pay from the treasury to the states banks for the common good to make sure our schools remain open, increasing the teaching staff, offering classes that meet the future business requirements, paying good salaries, offering student loans, increase tutoring, having parents engage with student activity or any new ideas to promote education as essential.

Medicare, medical, and the children's health care plan should be combined into one plan covering everyone.

Medical research programs should be increased. The states common good banks cover losses. Without health being a priority, everything else fails.

Roads have been crumbling and minimal patch work has been applied to keep them working. Being safe is the issue and reworking the entire road system is critical.

All *service priority jobs* in cities, territories, and states should be accomplished by money provided by the state banks for the common good to free up current budget problems. Once unemployment levels are established and money starts circulating, more tax could be collected to help future monetary problems.

Poverty should be a priority- It is absolutely critical to uplift everyone into a comfortable status. Food, housing, clothing, medical, education, jobs, and safety are essential. Banks for the common good in each state must provide money to move people from poverty.

*Research Money-*The largest challenge is medical research for the cure of cancer, diabetes, and other diseases. Scientists should start looking for ways of evaluating what has been done around the world.

Readjusting the tax situation- Taxes, or should we say tidings must be collected from everyone. That includes individuals and businesses. The percentages collected for everyone could be lowered. Some people have questioned if the *treasury* can print money and there is no debt, why have tax? If the U.S. provides money for the common good, then an expression of appreciation should be shown by everyone.

The Jail Population– There should be a way to evaluate the laws concerning incarceration. The cost of keeping people in jail is more than providing education. The population in jail is staggering. Multiple states should get together and establish one jail in a remote section of Alaska. Minimal coverage would be required and the cost of incarceration would be lowered. Rehabilitate minor offenders and have them work for the common good.

Classes and Jobs for everyone– Creating jobs and getting the money circulated would now get this country out of this recession. It is critical for everyone to take charge and change those in congress to adapt to a new monetary (money) and budget systems. At the present time only a few of those in congress are knowledgeable about macro or micro economics. It should be a priority for not only congress, but everyone to take classes to understand basic economics.

All the following topics will discuss actions regarding money. Every action taken by an individual, company, city, state or government affects the economy and problems that occur in this society at the present time. When you read the following topics put yourself into the ideas how these topics affect you and your family now, or in the future.

The next topic brings up the largest problem facing this country since the end of the Second World War. <u>*Outsourcing*</u> has stripped the country of manufacturing causing lack of competition due to cheap external labor. If we were to compete, wages would have to be lowered that diminishes the buying of goods and services by middle class. The following is the explanation of what has occurred over the years.

Chapter 9 – Outsourcing, Deregulation, Scams, and Greed

Fighting Small Business and Employees

Let's go back a few years and discuss money problems and the working conditions affecting millions of people. After the Second World War the Marshall Plan, named after General George Marshall, moved the latest technology of steel production to Germany and Japan to rebuild those countries. Within a short time those foreign countries imported finished steel products to the United States at prices <u>way below</u> the cost of similar products produced here.

The importing was gradual at first and no one really started thinking that it would create problems. *The government didn't take any steps*-- such as adding tariffs to even out the playing field or by getting those foreign countries to increase their employees' salaries and improve living standards for their employees. By doing that the foreign countries employees would be able to buy their own products they are selling, and create a much more even competition of products made here.

Competition is desirable as it increases quality and lowers prices. Unfortunately importing and later outsourcing was the biggest problems that started the greatest downfall of businesses in Pennsylvania, West Virginia, Ohio, and many of the neighboring states.

Many businesses couldn't compete with comparable imported goods at lower prices. Without knowing what to do, they either closed their doors or decided to move their production of goods offshore where labor costs are extremely small. That was the start of outsourcing as we know it today.

Besides the steel companies many industries were delighted as they started moving their production companies offshore bypassing high labor costs and to lower corporate taxes. As technology increased, businesses found they needed fewer employees to accomplish their needs. The labor market started to dry up. Pensions disappeared, unemployment reached a peak with thousands unemployed. Towns and cities were starting to crumble. Deregulation later came into effect for banks and brokerage companies. Wages along with unions were starting to disappear.

Outsourcing is global. If our country is in a recession because many people are out of work and buy only necessary products to survive, it may affect the outsourcing country. Countries that have lower living standards with employees working on slave labor conditions with the inability to buy their own products, may find their country in a depression.

The next topic talks about the housing market and the security market scams. Market deregulation since the time of President Regan started the collapse of the housing market and the many ponzi scams in the security market and banking, started the greatest fall of the economy since the 1930's. Our deregulation even affects the foreign market.

Deregulation and Greed

The security market and housing market over the years took advantage of everyone by the biggest loss of money since the great depression. This is what happened.

Scams and greed

Deregulation of the housing and security market started the devastating idea of ruining retirement and pension funds and caused bankruptcies and mortgage defaults. Banks and brokerage houses started hedge funding, and all types of scams and ponzi schemes. Bernie Madoff had the largest ponzi scheme (an investment fraud that involves the payment of purported returns to existing investors from funds contributed by new investors) in the history of the United States that affected thousands of people costing billions of dollars.

In fact from 1992 to 2008 the S.E.C. eight times investigated Madoff. The agency came away with nothing and ignored a detailed letter it received in 2005 from a Boston-based investor Harry Markopoulos titled "The World's Biggest Hedge Fund Is a Fraud." The managing director of hedge funds at Neuberger Berman stated - to protect you the following basic checks on all investments should include:

Audited financial statements from a recognized accountant- Independent confirmation that securities were traded at the prices claimed- Independent custodian who holds the assets of a company to prove they actually exist- An unbelievable amount of due diligence in the management firm before you put up any money- Stress-testing the trading strategy and talking to the auditors- <u>Of course this information is after the problems occurred. Too bad it wasn't done before.</u>

For the most part, hedge funds (unlike mutual funds) are unregulated because they cater to sophisticated investors. In the U.S., laws require that the majority of investors in the fund be accredited. That is, they must earn a minimum amount of money annually and have a net worth of more than $1 million, along with a significant amount of investment knowledge.

You can think of hedge funds as mutual funds for the super-rich. They are similar to mutual funds in that investments are pooled and professionally managed, but differ in that the fund has far more flexible in its investment strategies.

It is important to note that hedging is actually the practice of attempting to reduce risk, but the goal of most hedge funds is to maximize return on investment. The name is mostly historical, as the first hedge funds tried to hedge against the downside risk of a bear market by shorting the market (mutual funds generally can't enter into short positions as one of their primary goals). Nowadays, hedge funds use dozens of different strategies, so it isn't accurate to say that hedge funds just "hedge risk." In fact, because hedge fund managers make speculative investments, these funds can carry more risk than the overall market.

Bear market —A prolonged period in which investments prices fall, accompanied by widespread pessimism.

Short selling - The selling of a security that the seller does not own, or any sale that is completed by the delivery of a security borrowed by the seller. Short sellers assume that they will be able to buy the stock at a lower amount than the price at which they sold short.

Most of the scams were in the housing mortgage market. Fraud was prevalent and one day the housing mortgage market bubble collapsed. Brokerage companies collapsed. We were heading for another depression. At the end of 2008 the economy declined into the worst recession where the security market fell 50% in less than a month. Nothing like this has occurred since the great depression of the 1930's. Millions of businesses and jobs were lost. Many people lost their homes. Many pension funds, IRA's and 401K funds were depleted by the largest down market. With all the problems caused by the security market and mortgage market changes had to be done to protect everyone.

Chapter 10 – Changes Taking Place

When the Democrats Controlled Congress

In 2008 the Democratic Party with a Democratic president took control of the House and Senate. The government had to step in to shore up the banks and brokerage firms and other businesses to keep the economy going.

Bills were being passed to: Safeguard the unemployed by extending unemployment insurance, protect consumers against credit card companies gouging of interest rates, allowing millions to be covered by health insurance even with pre-existing conditions and offsetting huge price increases by health insurance companies, fixing problems with Medicare and Medical by closing the doughnut hole relieving seniors of paying exorbitant fees, regulating the banks and brokerage companies from getting into businesses that caused huge money losses for everyone, loaning money to small businesses so they can create new jobs, creating new jobs and green jobs to start getting away from imported oil, fighting the British Petroleum Corporation causing the largest oil explosion and leak that created the largest environmental disaster in the United States and Gulf of Mexico due mainly to bypassing stringent environmental controls, lowering the tax burden for the middle class and letting the tax breaks for those making over $250,000 per year to expire, safeguard the unemployed by extending unemployment insurance. The best idea to stimulate the economy would be for the government to <u>add tariffs</u> to even out the playing field from those business and countries that bring in products from overseas that offset United States labor costs.

Quality products can be produced here offering competition and creating new jobs. All these new changes now lead to the idea of advising you how to take charge of different situations where <u>you</u> can maintain control of your destiny.

The Next Topic will discuss ideas to help individuals and businesses succeed. The ideas being presented are ideas from around the world. Sometimes those ideas could be beneficial to your business.

Chapter 11 – Thinking Outside the Box

Finding New Ideas

This makes a person more appreciative of possible changes in their daily lives. Thinking and taking charge of new ideas is hard, but we have to be <u>proactive</u> in moving our thoughts forward.

<u>Proactive</u> is acting in advance to deal with an expected difficulty; anticipatory, relating to, caused by, or being interference between previous learning and the recall or performance of later learning such as acting in anticipation of future problems, needs, or changes.

The following is an example of a TV show on July 28th 2000 I hosted, where the topic was Northridge, California Kiwanis. My guest was a friend of mine from Northridge Kiwanis. We discussed the reasons why we both joined the organization and I was very impressed why he joined.

He stated that most people question why "they" should do something instead of "I" should do something. He said that this organization offers each individual a key toward expressing the desire to achieve something in a collective way. The expression that nothing gets achieved until one decides to "step up to the plate" And do something is correct. If everyone just talks about doing something, nothing gets accomplished.

Success depends upon action- Most people are not proactive. As society progresses and the ability to obtain the items we desire becomes easier, being proactive starts to disappear. Starting from the late 1800's the majority of people that came to the United States had to make adjustments to the new society and new ways of living. Many family members were used to running a small business, where the adults of the family would encourage their children to learn the family business.

With the start of the Industrial revolution, people were encouraged to move from the rural areas of America to the cities and toward companies that promised jobs, good pay, a chance to advance, and above all loyalty.

The drift toward company jobs took away self-expression, family cohesiveness, and the ability to solve business and financial problems, and the ability of being proactive, expressed in the way businesses tell an individual --- How much a person is to be paid, --- When they can go on vacation, --- What kind of work they will perform, --- Where and when they will work.

The incentive to be one's own person and to make decisions is now in the hands of others. The company has the final say when it comes for --- Promotion, --- Switching schedules, ---telling you when you will retire, --

- or being released because of downsizing. If anyone wants to get ahead in the companies, they "must not buck" the politics of the company management.

When you are trying for a salary increase, have you expressed a percentage or dollar amount you desire? The majority of people just "let things happen" and don't want to "buck "their boss because he controls their jobs.

Learn how to control – Starting slowly when one wants to become proactive. It is a bit scary at first because you are not sure what will happen. What is the worst case scenario when asking for a raise? You don't get what you think you should get. The Boss said NO. <u>Of course if you didn't ask for what you want, don't blame anyone but yourself.</u>

Without asking, you let things happen to you. If you feel that you should get a bigger raise, maybe it is time to have your resume handy. There are always organizations that are willing to pay you what you desire.

Many company organizations lost their loyalty toward their employees. If you feel that you should be getting promotions, increases in salaries etc., you better start taking action. It is absolutely amazing when someone becomes proactive. The ability to achieve more and to demand and get what you desire seems to just happen. It is as if you "stepped out of yourself" and observed and controlled the world around you.

You become broader in your approach to achieving your goals. Learn to control instead of being controlled. Being proactive requires taking charge.

Some businesses ideas - If you own a business or thinking of starting a business the following would help you think differently. Some of the ideas are for those that want to start a business or already have a business. Checks and balances are needed for working with your employees and customers. About half of all small businesses fail within the first four years. This statistic could generate a shudder of fear in even the most dauntless entrepreneur. Most of these failures, however, resemble one another in crucial ways. And once you identify these harbingers of failure, you can increase your own chance of success.

Procrastination- When you own a small business; you will find that tasks and paperwork pile up like snowdrifts on your desk. Putting them off is like piling up debt; eventually they could overwhelm you.

Ignoring the competition- Consumer loyalty has declined sharply in recent years. Today, customers go where they can find the best products and services, even if that means breaking off long-term business relationships. Monitor your competitors, and don't be ashamed to copy their best ideas (assuming that doesn't mean violating patent law). Better yet, devote some time each week or month to devising new methods, products or services for your firm.

Sloppy or ineffective marketing- Contrary to the popular cliché, few products or services "sell themselves." If you don't have time to market your product effectively, hire an experienced person to do it for you. Marketing keeps your products selling and money flowing into your business. It's crucial that you do it well.

Ignoring customers´ needs- Once you attract customers, you'll have to work hard to keep them. Customer service should be a key aspect of your business. If you don't follow through with your customers, they'll find someone who will.

Incompetent employees- Hire only workers who are essential to your operation. When you do hire employees, make sure they're well trained and able to complete the tasks expected of them, and remember that happy employees make good workers. Try to create a work environment that keeps your staff happy and motivated.

Lack of versatility- You may be great at making hats or painting houses or fixing computers, but that's not enough to make your millinery shop or house painting business or computer consultancy successful. Successful business owners tend to be adept at a number of tasks, from accounting to marketing to hiring.

Poor location- Even the best restaurant or retail store will fail if it's in the wrong place. When you're scouting a location for your firm, consider factors such as traffic (how many potential customers pass your firm during the course of an afternoon or evening?) and convenience (how hard is it for your regular customers to get to your location on a regular basis?).

Cash flow problems- You need to know how to track the money coming into and out of your business -- even a profitable venture will flounder if it runs short of cash. In addition, you must learn to make cash flow projections that will help you decide how much money you can afford to spend and warn you of impending trouble.

A closed mind- Everyone goes into business with some preconceptions don't be surprised if you find that many of yours are wrong. Look for mentors who can give you advice and run your ideas by them before you make important financial commitments. Read books and magazines about small business, visit business-related Web sites and network with your peers in the business community.

Inadequate planning- Start with realistic but precise goals for your firm, including deadlines. For example: Don't just say that you want to increase sales; instead, decide that you want sales to reach $100,000 by next holiday season. Then write down the steps you can take to meet those goals on time, and set deadlines for completing those steps. Consult your goal list every day, and make sure you are doing what you need to do to meet your objectives.

Rethinking your business in crucial times

A better idea for your business is in critically looking at the large failures in business today due to the largest recession since the 1930's – and ask yourself the following questions as if you are a customer looking at your business:

For an individual or business in today's society you have to think outside the box. Ask the following for you or your business all the time. Why would I want to use your services? What makes you different then your competition?

A new approach for your resume

You might want to start thinking and writing about this immediately, but I would suggest you follow the next information regarding what you would put on your resume to get some ideas that work. The ideas presented on the resume to an individual out of work for quite a period of time, could be used to improve your business advertisement and gaining a clearer thought to outperform your competition.

What would you put on your resume- In taking classes at a local university and during a break I started conversing with an individual in the hallway. Being inquisitive, I asked what he did. He stated that he was out of work for almost a year. I asked him how his resumes were working. He stated not good and he tried everything and got no response.

I suppose you probably put everything on your resume what you did in the past? Companies today have stacks of resumes about four feet thick and only have time to skim them. How about this idea? <u>Find information from the internet of companies that interest you, and find out what you can do for them</u>. List those ideas on your resume as the first thing, and the last thing on that list would be "<u>That is why you should hire me.</u>" That sounds aggressive, but it works. This idea is extremely proactive- and would be viewed by those reading your resume first thing.

Why wouldn't someone call you for an appointment? As an owner of a company that needed workers and finding a resume that looked like that, they would be foolish not to call you for an appointment? In fact, you stepped up, being proactive, and taking charge of your resume by asking to be hired. You might be just the person the company could use as a manager and not for the job for which you are applying.

My friend in the hallways stated that the idea was very weird in putting this information on the resume. I stated your resumes didn't work so what is the worst thing that could happen if you changed your resume and went on an interview? All they could say is NO and you had a lot of them already.

The next week we met during a break, and he said, I want to thank you for what for you told me what to do and because of that I got myself a job. I got a tingling sensation, knowing that the idea worked differently than anything else.

Think back to those two questions asked regarding businesses, and use the above scenario of the resume in designing fliers for your business with the thoughts of <u>why would I want to use your services and what makes you different than your competition?</u>

Running for Political Office

Expand your thoughts if you look at the idea of running for a political office. At a convention I attended I managed to talk to thirty people running for political office. I read their literature, listening to their ideas, and none of them used the ideas of what they would do for the people they want to represent, and they never asked for the vote. <u>What was specified was what was done in the past, and a listing of their endorsements.</u>

In presented them the idea of being unemployed, looking for work, and mentioned having a job for them. With four feet of resumes and 4 seconds to review their resume they were asked" <u>what would you put on your resume to entice me to call you?"</u>

It actually is amazing that in talking to over thirty different people you would think they would have ideas of thinking what is for the common good, and would come forward with their ideas. They all wanted to tell me of things in the past and others mentioned that, so why would I vote for you? When bringing up different ideas they could see they needed a change in their oral and written presentations.

One of the ideas brought up was the idea of knowing who their competition is -- and understanding how their completion thinks. Once that is known, then why would anyone want to vote for your competition, when you know what they know, plus what you know?

What the difference is-- the question of what makes you different than your competition, and why would I vote for you? All brochures should use what is called the "kiss principle," keep it short and simple. Use the idea in designing them, and remember the average person only has <u>four seconds</u> to read a message. The message should be what you are going to do for them, and asking them to vote for you.

Keep away from half-truths (discussed later in the book) or bad mouthing someone. Telling the truth does not need a constant requirement of always telling falsehoods. Those that believe in falsehoods can't fool all the people all the time and can't be trusted. Truth and trust go hand in hand for your future.

As was stated before you have to open up to new ideas to move you toward the common good. Think carefully about each statement. You may want to add your own ideas.

The Next Topic- food for thought consists of short statements giving ideas for self-improvement. It is another way to maintain an attitude of being proactive.

Food for Thought

Learn how to accumulate significant wealth by minimizing your realized/taxable income and maximizing your unrealized/nontaxable income.

Education means development of the mind so that it will work for you and not against you. All education is self-acquired because no one can educate another.

If you don't know what you want, don't say you never had a chance.

A Master Mind Alliance is defined as "coordination of knowledge and effect, in a spirit of perfect harmony, between two or more people, for the attainment of a common definite purpose."

The first step toward a successful Master Mind Alliance is to get on terms with you. Do some master minding with your other self so you become thoroughly acquainted with who you are. It takes courage to face the truth.

When the spirit of teamwork is willing, voluntary, and free, it leads to the attainment of great and enduring power.

Don't waste your time on people who form opinions before examining the evidence.

If your purpose is worthy and your pursuit of it sincere, you'll have the courage to act decisively, gaining for yourself the things others see only in their dreams.

An hour of practical experience may be worth a year of theoretical training.

Hopeful wishing is a good starter, but a poor finisher. Think with a Positive Mental Attitude, and follow through with desirable action.

You must have faith to succeed, because if you're without faith, you're without hope.

Take possession of your mind and worry will have to find another boarding house.

Ponder the fact that you have complete control over but one thing, and that is the power of your own thoughts.

Everything you need or want has a way of showing up as soon as you are ready for it. Set a goal-and set it high-then keep trying until you achieve it-

The habit of always going the extra mile is an invaluable asset that will repay you much more than the effort spent.

Indecision and procrastination are twin brothers. Where one is found, the other may usually be found.

If you know your own mind, you know to always keep it positive. You can't become the master of anything or anyone until you become the master of your own ego.

The Next Topic business planning uses creative ideas from a CPA. The main emphasis is working with ideas to help businesses succeed.

Business Planning

There are many businesses that fail. One of my friends is a CPA and contributed this information. Ben Karimi, Certified Public Accountant, Encino, CA stated that if you are self-employed, make sure that you do not put all your money into your business. If your business fails, and you have separate savings, you will then have some emergency money.

He stated that he talked to many people that are trying to establish a business and decide to put all their money into the business. He warned them that many businesses fail because of lack of capital and a "slowing down" of business. He mentioned that bankruptcy has increased, and many could have been avoided, if there was a business plan.

Business plan information can be found on the Internet if you have a computer with a modem. The way of finding the latest information is to search the web by using the find command. Enter "business plan" or "small business association" and the search programs will give you a choice of plans and very good advice. If you don't have a computer I suggest that you can telephone the "small business administration" or visit your local library.

One of the important features of starting a business is to have enough money to keep the business going for a minimum of six months. The following are some of the reasons why a six-month supply of money is necessary.

You open your door, and no one shows up. It takes time to establish clients and advertising. Advertising requires about three attempts before the clients start to know your business. Your business is seasonable and the business expenses never stop. According to your business plan, all necessary money ideas would have been established.

Most businesses fail because the customer, employees and sales persons are not treated respectfully or with courtesy. There are times when your days are not running smoothly and you feel tense. Don't forget that your tense feelings could be reflected toward your customers or worse yet toward your employees or sales persons.

I called a potential customer whose responsibility is a general manager for a large food chain. I have always respected this person and his responsibilities. One day when I called he gave me a run around and hung up on me. How do you think I felt? About a month later in recalling him I confronted him and asked him about being a manager and treating his customers or employees that way. The story that finally came out was that the company was being bought out and he was not sure if he was to maintain his job.

To be in business today you must be creative. I once recalled a few years ago that when my wife and I were driving home our car broke down. I called the Automobile Club to send someone. The problem couldn't be fixed so we had the car towed. We had the car fixed at the garage from the towing company and was dropped off at our home and later picked up the car.

About a week later we received a "Thank You" letter from the company that fixed the car. That was a real shock. Imagine getting a "thank you" letter from a garage. I was so impressed that I went back to the garage and told the owner how impressed I was and thanked him for his service. I found that the work was excellent, the place was clean, and to this day I always use their services.

If you either work for someone or own your own business, <u>remember that the products of the business belong to the business</u>. It may seem strange, <u>but the E-mail belongs to the business.</u> Never send personal notes via e-mail because it could be held against you and you wouldn't want to see the notes held up in an open courtroom.

The relationships between working personnel should be kept in a working manner. Remember the people working either for you or with you are really not your personal friends. You are there to do a job and to keep your thoughts about how you feel about others to yourself.

The main idea is to keep the business running smoothly without difficult relationships between personnel. These relationships may be between employees and their supervisors or among employees. If friction occurs, make a decision, take charge of the problem, and be responsive.

As I mentioned be responsive in your answers, and you should remember that the customer and salesperson are due respect. Put yourself in their shoes and make a <u>determination if you would use your own services.</u>

When you are in business, you must wear a "mask of pleasure" to protect you from yourself. After business hours, the mask can come off.

The Next Topic the inflation saving health plan will discuss ideas I had many years ago and just kept the article for this moment. This is a great sales tool concept that should be used by businesses today.

The Inflation Saving Health Plan (ISHP)

This idea came to me on October 7, 2000 before the credit card companies even thought of giving cash back. When you go to a grocery store, check out, waggle a special card, or give them your phone number, they give you a discount on marked products. Of course if you forgot the card or didn't give them your phone number you paid retail. In other words the discounts are worthless.

Why couldn't that discount be placed into a <u>bank or money market account or brokerage account "ear marked" as a special way of savings or for your health plan?</u> Granted, the discounts are given to the people as a way of purchasing products, but this idea is to make the money more valuable. Since the money is "ear marked" for special use, the likelihood of removing or spending the money would be slower.

What, you're going to get money to help with your savings account or health account from a store? Guess what, <u>the poor would have money</u>, or the earmarking for a health account could be worth more than the money.

What does it do for the banks? It gives them enough money to meet their payroll on Fridays, eliminating the need to borrow from the Federal Reserve. In other words, a "golden handshake" between the store and bank that evolves into a partnership on money borrowing. Banks and businesses should start this sales idea.

The Current Situations- The prevention of future increased inflation is the primary reason for the Federal Government to increase the interest rate. The Federal Government is trying to slow down an increase in consumer spending that causes price increases in goods and services. With increasing interest rates, business growth may stifle, which may cause more business bankruptcy.

Large companies that need to borrow funds to increase their growth will more than likely "pass off" the increased interest rate costs to the public. Smaller companies may have a more difficult time in borrowing funds and may not have the ability to increase the growth of their business or meet competition resulting in business failure.

The slowing down of the economy caused by businesses being stifled usually will cause an increase in unemployment. If unemployment increases, the amount of consumer spending decreases. With the decreasing of consumer spending, businesses are forced to lay off more people. The government hopes this will slow the economy. More governmental interest rate increases could cause a recession or depression.

The time involved from the increases of interest rates to the actual slowing down of the economy generally takes about a year before the effects are felt. Individuals that are working on a fixed or limited budget or forced out of employment will suffer. What the government doesn't understand is that the taxes collected from businesses would be less.

Medicare, Social Security and other programs are being affected by the reduction in tax collections. With higher costs to business, profits are less. Stock Prices usually decrease affecting everyone's portfolio. We have no control over the federal government except to find a way to control inflation. There must be a better way to offset inflation.

The Definition of Inflation- is a general and progressive increase in prices. Everything gets more valuable except money. Inflation is a persistent increase in the level of consumer prices or a persistent decline in the purchasing power of money, caused by an increase in available currency and credit beyond the proportion of available goods and services.

Health Saving & Problems- As I mentioned before, the money placed in the banks, money market or brokerage accounts should be "ear marked" for special functions such as inflation and Health Care. Everyone needs to have a means to cover the rising costs of health care. As the public ages, health costs escalate to the point that our average savings could be depleted.

The disadvantages that we face today are that the Health Care Plans that we buy today may not cover the eventual costs of medical or dental expenses in the near future. I know most people would not like to have a life style that is <u>LESS</u> than they have today.

A Different Idea- The first idea is to change the way of thinking by the public and business into thinking that inflation can't be controlled. The public must understand that Health Care moneys should now be collected for potential future needs. Everyone must be instructed that the method to offset and control inflation and collect moneys for Health Care is through savings and Controlled Spending.

There will always be inflation. But should the control be in the hands of the government or business? If in the hands of business, favoritism, fraud, etc. are eliminated for the most part, but harder to control. Granted, not everything in controlling inflation either by business or the government is exact. Mistakes will happen, but the object is to try to eliminate the lack of control, such as during the 1980's or the over doing of controlling methods used today. We don't have any voice in the way the inflation is controlled today. What other methods of correcting inflation or paying for Health Care are been tried here in the United States?

This idea is different and a great sales tool- Businesses today could control inflation and help pay health care costs through a simple method of "paying back Inflation to the public & saving for health care".

The public should recognize this "Paying Back" as an "Inflation saving/Health Plan (ISHP)" instead of business discounts. Granted, there is a tremendous learning curve by everyone. The average inflation over the years has been averaging about 4%. Percent are flexible & will vary as determined by the profit margin of merchandise being sold.

The illustrations will use 4%. Businesses buy their supplies and goods from their vendors. To start the process, the vendors will give to their business clients a 4% (ISHP) and the businesses that sell to their client will give a 4% (ISHP.)

Exclusions would be savings accounts or money market accounts. Money in these accounts could earn interest and would be tax free. Other exclusions could be prescription medicine, hospital bills, insurance, mortgages, rentals, licenses and taxes. There may be more exclusion as required. Alcohol and Tobacco products <u>should not</u> be excluded.

All non-excluded Products or Services purchased; the customer would receive 4% from the person, corporation, body politic, or governmental agency. All non-excluded Products or Services sold; the customer would pay 4% to the person, corporation, body politic or governmental agency. A <u>Body Politic</u> is the people of a politically organized nation or state considered as a group.

If there is a purchase or sale, and the item is taxable, the tax is calculated after subtracting the (ISHP). Here is an example: Purchase a product that has a value of $20.00 and receive a (ISHP) of 4% or $.80. The net is $19.20. The tax would be on $19.20. Sell a product that has a value of $25.00 and pay a (ISHP) of 4% or $1.00 for a net of $26.00. The tax would be on $25.00.

The (ISHP) Credit / Debit Card- I feel that each individual and business has the use of an (ISHP) Credit/Debit card tied to a bank, brokerage account, or money market account. The process could work very well. The money would be <u>automatically deposited</u> for those buying directly into the buyer's bank; savings or brokerage accounts, and <u>reduced</u> for those selling directly from the seller's bank, savings or brokerage accounts.

The money deposited in the bank, savings or brokerage accounts should grow tax deferred. The money reduced for the (ISHP) should be kept as a separate entry for future use. This is a better way of saving for a future benefit. Monthly reports should be generated to show the (ISHP) accounts. Only direct withdrawals from the (ISHP) account should be allowed.

Today, many of us use the withdraw system from our checking or savings accounts to pay for Insurance, car payments etc. I believe that most people would have to really think about really deciding to reduce the money in the (ISHP) account since money is automatically deposited and growing tax deferred and would begin to understand this is a terrific way to control inflation, and help to pay for Health Care in case of disaster. Everyone wins with automatic savings starting at a young age and paid by purchases.

Advantages of having an (ISHP) - **Everyone** would have a (ISHP) special account. Even the underprivileged people would have money. Money seems to solve many problems. The idea for having (ISHP) on security purchases would be to eliminate the gambling or day trading. The idea is to stabilize savings into more long-term investments. <u>If businesses wanted to increase prices, the customer would receive more (ISHP) money.</u>

The extra (ISHP) money received could be used for more savings or increased spending. The control of the (ISHP) would be the responsibility of the companies or government. If the (ISHP) percentage were decreased, there would be fewer savings and less spending by the customer and less borrowing capabilities by the Businesses. If the (ISHP) percentage were increased, there would be more savings and more spending by the customer.

Banks and brokerage houses would now have more money to lend at lower rates. Banks would not need to borrow from the FED to meet minimum requirements. Businesses could now borrow for expansion with "reasonable" rates. Expansion of businesses would increase productivity thereby offering more jobs, savings etc.

The controlled movement of the (ISHP) by business or government could control overspending or under-spending by the customers. This would also control the price of stock. If companies have to give out fewer dollars for the (ISHP), the stock price may rise due in part to increased earnings. On the other hand, an increase of the (ISHP) could cause the stock price to fall.

Problems and Comments- The lack of control by many people to overspend could cause shortages, and increased pressure on companies to produce more. Prices could escalate because of an increased spending of the (ISHP) and may cause runaway inflation. I believe that the buying frenzy could be controlled. Granted there are always people that would overspend, but the majority would not. The process of having businesses "gear up" for production understanding, if they give money away, they will also receive. What a great way for everyone to succeed.

What are Savings- When the great depression started during the 1930's, businesses, jobs and savings were lost. There was a run on the banks to withdraw money accumulated over the years, and many banks didn't have enough money to meet the demand.

Many banks closed their doors and never reopened. Overnight a number of people found themselves walking the streets in search of food, shelter and work. It was at this time people started to realize that money had to be diversified to be safe and guaranteed to be available for any emergency. This was the beginning of a true plan for savings.

The government stepped in and created jobs to help those in need to get reestablished. Many people were determined to start putting a portion of their earnings into savings for emergencies and retirement. Children were then taught the value of savings.

Look what is happening now? Did we learn from past experiences? What is in store for us in the future? Now is the time to start thinking differently.

The Next Topic will discuss the credit card. How the banks control everything including getting by the usury law.

The Credit Card

The first credit card was established in the 1950's. One of the first credit cards was offered by the Standard Oil Company. At that time, only business owners were eligible. They had to pay off the card in full each month. When someone drove into a gas station and presented their credit card, it was checked against a list of delinquent accounts. If that card's number appeared, the cardholder would be required to surrender his card. Thereafter he would be required to use cash for all purchases.

Other cards started to appear. The next card was offered by Sears. The difference was that the card owner wasn't just a business owner, but was the head of household. Bad credit started to appear. The credit card companies decided to charge interest.

A usury law was established *(Office of Attorney General, State of California, Department of Justice-http://ag.ca.gov/consumers/general/usury.php)* that stipulated that the amount of charges of interest or fees could not exceed ten percent of the unpaid monthly balance. The credit card companies and banks found a way around that law. Today many credit card interest rates are higher than 10 percent-- Way higher!!

Times were much simpler after the Second World War. There were not any credit cards, and purchases were made by paying cash. If you wanted something, you saved for it. There was not the number of savings options that exist today. Only a small percentage of people invested in the stock market, and most savings were with banks.

Business and credit cards- Businesses like credit cards because it makes purchasing more convenient and buying more immediate. Credit cards stimulated the production of new items-- such as household goods, furniture, clothes, cars, etc. -- and the "need" of ownership of those products. When television started to advertise new products, it stimulated a buying frenzy that continues today.

The problem is the credit card purchases often exceeded a person's income. The emergency money that had been saved was now used to pay the credit card balance. The banks and credit card companies stimulated the dangerous thinking of buy/charge today, pay tomorrow. Credit cards are fine, provided the cards are paid in full each month.

Credit Debt- One of the biggest obstacles to savings is credit card debt. The credit card companies charge interest on unpaid balances and stipulate on each monthly bill that a minimum amount of the outstanding balance is to be paid, instead of the outstanding balance that is due on the next bill.

The credit card companies suggest you pay only a minimum amount because they don't make any money when you pay your balance in full each month. Paying only the minimum due each month shortly became the standard practice or the norm, and the continuation of the debt.

What's happening today- With the outsourcing of jobs to other countries, the laying off of workers and the closing of many businesses over the last decade, there has been a decline in saving for emergencies. <u>In fact, this is the first time that the number of individuals saving has gone negative in the United States.</u>

This is an article from -(*Federal Reserve Board of San Francisco* <u>*http://www.frbsf.org/publications/economics/letter/2005/el2 005-30.html*</u>)

When considering job loss, the housing market fiasco, increased fuel prices, rising health costs, overspending, credit card debt, bankruptcy, destruction from hurricanes, tornadoes and floods, and

any promise of building a savings seems to disappear.

Who Needs to Save Money

A common complaint is that there isn't enough money left over each month to go to savings. The problems we all face over the years are a loss of our jobs and unexpected medical problems. What happens if you become disabled and unable to work? How would your lifestyle change if you were disabled, out of work or had medical problems that required a lot of money?

When you retire or the income from your job stops from a disability, where do you plan to get the money to pay your bills for the remainder of your lifetime? Are you expecting to receive a retirement bonus from your work, or do you have a disability policy that is tied to the cost-of-living so it increases each year? What have you planned in the way of savings?

How are you going to teach your children to save? Your children will learn their saving ideas from you. If you don't know how to save, do you expect your children to know how to save and keep away from costly mistakes? Where do you find the extra money to begin saving?

Saving Ideas- One thing I would suggest is to pay attention to where and how you spend your money on a daily basis. By making some changes, extra money can be available to you each month.

If you are buying coffee at work or on your way to work, you are spending a huge amount of money every month. I suggest you invest in the least expensive coffee grinder and grind your own. The French Press is not expensive, and easy to use and clean. Take a thermos of coffee to work. Do the math: you may be spending $2.00 to $5.00 a day or $40.00 to $100.00 a month on that gourmet coffee that you buy outside. Make your own coffee at home at a cost of $8.00 - $14.00 a month and you'll save $32.00 - $86.00. That amounts to hundreds of dollars over the course of a year.

Another <u>very expensive</u> item is bottled water. If you use it, buy the least expensive product and the largest size. You can always store the water in smaller containers for your personal use. Another savings idea is to purchase items by the case. This is especially true with drinking water, paper products, non-perishables, etc.

<u>When dining out,</u> you might want to consider the cost of purchasing alcohol beverages. You may be spending $6.00 to $9.00 for a glass of wine or $48.00 to $72.00 for the bottle. That same wine bought in the store would cost you about $12.00 to $20.00 per bottle, and that would save you about $36.00 to $52.00.

Another good idea is to use store coupons. Be selective in your purchases; don't buy something just because it is on sale. A very key issue is to evaluate your credit card purchases before buying. Learn to question the "real need" for your purchase. This could represent a substantial savings; not only on the purchase itself, but on the interest on the unpaid balances.

Make a list of what you purchase, and see if there is extra money that can be set aside for your savings. You might be surprised as to the amount of money that you waste each month. If your job or business offers you the option of special savings, take advantage of it.

This book will help you to set up priorities for your savings. What will also be discussed is setting goals for savings, and how to achieve those goals.

The Next Topic will discuss the idea of making you a priority. It is very critical especially when starting to save money.

The Priority System

The only way to start saving is to <u>make yourself a priority</u>, just as if you were a bill to be paid each month. We always think of paying the telephone, water and power, gas, mortgage, car, clothing, food, dry cleaning, and other expenses first; but it never occurs to us to pay ourselves. The only way we can successfully save is to make ourselves a priority. We need to pay ourselves first and take care of our bills second.

Putting money aside every month <u>must become a habit</u>, just as waking up every morning when the alarm goes off, getting out of bed, getting dressed, having breakfast, etc. When you make yourself a priority, your goals become the reason to save.

Evaluate where to save- The bank savings account, money market, CD's, mutual funds, stock, the IRA, the Roth IRA, the SEP IRA, the Simple IRA, the 401K Plan, the 403B Plan, municipal bonds, annuities, and cash value life insurance are just a few ideas.

Short-medium-long term savings- The bank savings account, money market, and CD's would be considered <u>short-term savings products.</u> All of these types of savings offer a small amount of interest that may have restrictions or penalties, do not beat inflation, and are taxed.

The municipal bond and mutual funds would be considered <u>medium-term savings products.</u> There generally is <u>not any control</u> on the securities that are purchased. The municipal bonds are sensitive to interest rate movement daily, and the mutual funds are sensitive to the security market each day. The mutual funds are taxable.

Other savings ideas such as IRA's, Stock, Annuities, plus the mutual fund and the municipal bonds, would be considered <u>long-term savings</u>. Many have restrictions, penalties and are taxed.

As you continue reading about the different savings ideas, make decisions as the best, most convenient method for you. <u>You also should evaluate your savings plans yearly to determine if changes are needed in terms of the amount of money being saved, the length of time involved, and the priority of the savings.</u>

Take a picture and set a goal- The first thing you should do is to take a picture of the goal or a representation of it. Perhaps you want to go to Hawaii; you could pick up a travel brochure for your inspiration.

The second step is to make a list on how to plan and accomplish your goal. The outline should contain ideas about the amount of money to put aside each month, and also a time period for how long the goal should take. Make <u>three copies</u> of your list and the picture or representation thereof. Put one copy on the refrigerator, another on the mirror in the bathroom, and take the third to work so you can see it all day long.

What is on the paper- The first item on the paper is the goal. In other words, what is <u>the need for the money?</u>

The second item is <u>the time frame in which to obtain that goal</u>. That goal period will fluctuate during the saving period because of different priorities that may arise. The third item is <u>the amount of money you are determined to save</u> each month. This amount may change because of your need money during the savings period. The forth item is <u>where to save the money?</u>

Controlling the money- When applying money toward your savings, <u>keep a running total as you add money toward the goal.</u> Obtain a statement monthly and retain it with your goal papers. There may be times when there is not sufficient money to apply toward the goal, but <u>don't skip a payment, no matter how small the amount.</u>

<u>The easiest way to save is to set up an automatic withdrawal from a checking account.</u> At first the money withdrawn may make you feel uncomfortable, but it will soon become a habit. Every few months <u>reevaluate your goal</u> to determine if there has been any change in the cost of obtaining it. This would obviously shift the goal time period.

Your success in achieving your goal will be assured if you observe the picture of your goal and read the paper on a daily basis. Keep your goals in your mind's eye will help to keep you focused and on-track.

The urge to quit- Periodically there may be the urge or desire to borrow from your savings to pay off some other bills or to meet an emergency. Before doing so, reevaluate and prioritize to determine how critical is your savings? As your confidence in your savings plan grows, start thinking of larger, more long-term goals you may want to achieve in the future. Medium-term goals have a range from one to three years. Long-term goals are longer than three years.

Working and saving with children- <u>Children learn their ideas about saving money from their parents</u>. Of course, if the parents don't have a way of saving, how can they expect their children to learn? Teaching children the value of saving should start in kindergarten and then continue through college. It is not only the concept of savings, but money managing in general is the idea of keeping a checkbook in balance, working on a family budget, etc. If children learn early about the pitfalls of credit purchases, their outlook for future savings will improve.

The Next Topic will discuss the rules to saving. Follow the rule to keep away from mistakes. By continuing your saving and rules you start to learn how to take charge of your destiny. Habits are hard to break.

The Rule to Savings

The most important aspect of savings is the preservation of your money and its future growth. How would you like a savings that offered a guarantee that you would never lose a dime, but you would continue to accrue money better than any traditional savings account?

The problem is there are numerous plans that are not only risky, but impose penalties should you withdraw any of your savings before a specified period of time. Some of the plans charge what is called "surrender fees" that would give you less than you saved.

From the Merriam-Webster dictionary- surrender is: to give up completely or agree to forgo.

To give you an idea of the ramifications of not having a guaranteed savings: imagine after two years of putting money aside, the market drops and you lose $500 of your $1,000, which is a common scenario in today's market.

To get your savings back on track and earn back the $500 you lost, with no additional gain, it would take 14.4 years-- and that's if you earn an average 5 percent interest. You would actually have to earn 36 percent to make your money back in two years. Can you afford this extremely high risk?

You will be presented choices on different savings vehicles. Examine the advantages and disadvantages of each according to your risk tolerance and make a decision as to which will better meet your goal.

Don't fall into the trap of buying what you're saving for <u>before</u> there is money to pay for it. In today's credit-oriented world, it is far too easy to buy now and pay later. Once you learn the technique of saving, then you can start thinking about medium and long-term goals.

The Next Topic will discuss goals. A good part of being proactive is setting goals and working to accomplish something.

What are Goals

From the Merriam-Webster dictionary: a goal is, the end toward which effort is directed.

This book will discuss the short-term, medium-term, and long-term goals you will use for your savings.

Short-term goal—*From Wikipedia, the online encyclopedia - Short-term goals expect accomplishment in a short period of time, such as trying to get a bill paid in the next few days. The definition of a short-term goal need not relate to any specific length of time. In other words, one may achieve (or fail to achieve) a short-term goal in a day, week, month, year, etc. The time-frame for a short-term goal relates to its context in the overall timeline that it is being applied to. For instance, one could measure a short-term goal for a month-long project in days.*

*Establish short-term goals—*A short-term goal is used to save for a purchase that is made within a month to a year's time. This expenditure might be a short, little vacation or some new clothes.

For the short-term goals, the tendency would be to use a short-term money market, a bank savings (FDIC), or a Certificate of Deposit (CD) account. All of these are capable of ready conversion into cash, offering you easy access to your money. These methods offer some increase in profits, but that increase is taxable; and as we learned, taxing our money increases the time span involved in our savings plan. Please note: The CD has a penalty clause for any money withdrawn before the expiring time period.

Short-term emergency money- Due to the various uncertainties of life, (accidents, job loss, medical problems, damages from acts of nature, etc.) one of the most important aspects of our savings plan is to have an emergency fund that will cover at least six months to a year of our monthly expenses.

Not as fun or eagerly anticipated as that savings for our Hawaiian vacation, it offers the peace of mind that one good emergency won't lose you your home or lifestyle. Your savings should be placed where it can be accessed quickly.

Medium-term goals- are from one to three years. *From Kiplinger.com - S*afety is still important for your savings, but you are in a better position to ride out bad times in the financial markets and take on a little more risk. For medium-term goals, consider longer-term CDs that pay more interest than the short-term certificates you would buy to help finance your vacation trip. You might even consider mutual funds that pay good dividends but don't tend to fluctuate much in price. This could give you high income (for reinvesting in more fund shares); a chance to ride along if the market zooms, and pretty good protection against all but a steep drop in stock prices.

Medium-term goals would be those for such purchases as a down-payment on a car, furniture, fixtures, paintings, cruises, sporting equipment, office equipment, computers, printers, computer software, small business purchases, etc.

Some medium-term savings options- a money market account, CDs, (certificates of deposit) or a mutual fund. CDs can be taken out for different time periods. There is a disadvantage of a penalty if the money is required before the expiration date. CDs offer simple interest and are taxable.

The Next Topic will discuss calculating interest. Make a card and put this information on a card or on a notepad on your computer or phone. It becomes a great service when checking interest on purchases using your credit card.

Calculating Interest

From:
http://www.getobjects.com/Components/Finance/TVM/iy.html

Interest is the cost of borrowing money. An interest rate is the cost stated as a percent of the amount borrowed per period of time, usually one year. Simple interest is calculated on the original principal only. Accumulated interest from prior periods is not used in calculations for the following periods.

Simple interest- Simple interest is normally used for a single period of less than a year, such as 30 or 60 days.

For the formulas use   (x) = multiply and   (/) = divide

Simple Interest = p (x) i (x) n

Where:
p = principal (original amount borrowed or loaned)

 i = interest rate for one period

 n = number of periods

Example: You borrow $10,000 for 3 years at 5 percent simple annual interest.

Interest = p (x) i (x) n = $10,000 (x) .05 (x) 3 = $1,500

Example 2: You borrow $10,000 for 60 days at 5 percent simple interest per year (assume a 365 day year).

Interest = p (x) i (x) n = $10,000 (x) .05 (x) (60 (/) 365) = $82.1917

Compound Interest- Compound interest is calculated each period on the original principal and all interest accumulated during past periods. Although the interest may be stated as a yearly rate, the compounding periods can be yearly, semiannually, quarterly, or even continuously. You can think of compound interest as a series of back-to-back simple interest contracts. The interest earned in each period is added to the principal of the previous period to become the principal for the next period.

For example, you borrow $10,000 for three years at 5 percent annual interest compounded annually:

Interest year 1 = p (x) i (x) n = $10,000 (x) .05 (x) 1 = $500

Interest year 2 = (p_2 = p_1 (+) i_1) (x) i (x) n = ($10,000 (+) $500) (x) .05 (x) 1 = $525

Interest year 3 = (p_3 = p_2 (+) i_2) (x) i (x) n = ($10,500 (+) $525) (x).05 (x) 1 = $551.25

Total interest earned over the three years = $500 (+) $525 (+) $551.25 = $1,576.25. Compare this to $1,500 earned over the same number of years using simple interest.

The power of compounding- can have an astonishing effect on the accumulation of wealth. This table shows the results of making a one-time investment of $10,000 for 30 years using 12 percent simple interest, and 12 percent interest compounded yearly and quarterly.

Type of Interest	Principal Plus Interest Earned
Simple	$46,000.00
Compounded Yearly	$299,599.22
Compounded Quarterly	$347,109.87

The Next Topic will discuss mutual funds. This is the easiest way of saving where the risks are smaller. Being able to choose the right fund to match your risk tolerance is critical.

Mutual Funds

The funds invest money in a diversified group of companies or the securities of other corporations. The care in choosing any mutual fund is of primary concern because of the limited time involved in the fund. Expenses must be taken into consideration would be the purchasing and perhaps selling of the fund because the fund prices could be less than the original purchase.

Another consideration would be the daily price movement of the fund. You are always looking for positive results, but there is a chance that the fund might not produce a gain over a three-year medium-term plan period and the resulting outcome could be a loss.

Dollar-cost averaging- occurs when you buy shares at the current price and continue to purchase shares over a long period of time. Prices could be higher or lower over the period of time, thereby smoothing out the loss and gain in the fund price. If the fund price is less, more funds would be bought than when the fund price is higher.

From Wikipedia the on-line encyclopedia –Dollar cost averaging is a saving technique intended to reduce exposure tohttp://en.wikipedia.org/wiki/Risk risk associated with making a single large purchase.

The idea is simple: spend a fixed dollar amount at regular intervals (e.g., monthly) on a particular savings or portfolio/part of a portfolio, regardless of the share price. In this way, more shares are purchased when prices are low and fewer shares are bought when prices are high. The premise of dollar cost averaging is that the saver wants to guard against the market losing value shortly after making his savings. Therefore, he chooses to spread his savings over a number of periods. Since the market has a positive mean rate of return, dollar cost averaging usually requires the saver to give up some expected return for the benefit of reduced variance in his eventual outcome.

In fact, research has shown that saving a onetime large dollar amount according to these principles generally results in worse performance as compared to saving the entire sum at separate times.

However, the saver can expect a reduction in the variance of his performance by implementing dollar cost averaging. While dollar cost averaging can help to limit the downside of a worst-case scenario of an immediate drop in the value after the onetime large dollar amount is saved, most market research has shown that such drop-offs are relatively rare compared to the strong emphasis the strategy puts on avoiding them.

Municipal bond funds - Another alternative would be a municipal bond fund. The advantage to this type of fund would be the dividends paid out monthly and then incorporated back into the fund to purchase more funds. A municipal bond fund is TAX-FREE, whereas other mutual funds are taxable. Mutual funds will generally offer higher returns for the money.

The Next Topic will discuss the long term goals. Since a lot of ideas for savings use mutual funds and municipal bond funds, an understanding of short term goals and long term goals is required.

Long-Term Goals

Long-term goals are savings goals you expect to be accomplished in three years or longer. The type of savings plans are the IRA's, mutual funds, municipal bonds, annuities, stock, and life insurance. These long-term goals would be for such savings as:

Tuition for college

Down payment on a house

Start up for a business

Home remodeling

Large medical expenses

Disability

Retirement

Estate planning

Loss of work and unemployment

Accidents

Long Term Care Savings

Taking care- Before you determine the type of savings, evaluate different options and different companies to get the best offer. Don't be sold unless you completely understand the terms of your savings vehicle. Before signing any contract, have your CPA or financial advisor review the contracts.

The Next Topic will discuss selling; being proactive and making decisions will give you the opportunity to being more successful.

Selling, Being Proactive, and Making Decisions

Learning how to take charge of your sales you must understand that most people are not proactive and can't make decisions. You may hear all kinds of excuses, but the most used is *"I'll call you."* *What they are really saying is a polite way of saying NO.*

I really don't know where the idea of using the telephone as a "Polite Way of Saying NO" started. As a sales person I learned to accept rejection, when I was fortunate enough to present my ideas, products and concepts to "potential customers." The idea of being proactive and making decisions in my live made me realize that many people ARE NOT proactive and decision makers, and will use different methods of saying "NO." This method "of pushing you aside" is used "to not offend you" instead of being straightforward.

As an example, I would present some idea, concept, or product to a "potential customer" and their response would be, "I'm not sure, I'll call you." This answer is not a positive "yes or no." Since I am proactive and a decision maker, I have always thought that other people would be proactive and decision makers.

In so thinking, I always expected people to call. I generally would ask when the call would occur, and I would get the answer," shortly." Of course the calls never occurred. Did they "lie" to me or worse yet, did they lie to themselves. I on the other hand would have generally "chased" the "potential customer" in the belief that this "potential customer "would finally use my services. I generally felt that to be in business that I did not want to "dwindle down" my "potential lists."

Today, if I were to examine my "potential lists" and were to categorize them, I would find that the majority of my "potential lists" are starting to make decisions.

I Learned a Different Sales Technique: What I learned and what you can apply now is to tell the "potential customer", if I am given "I'll call you" response, is to say that, "I'll call you" is a polite way of saying "NO." Is that what you are telling me?

This offers "YOU" control of the situation. If the "potential customer" says, "That's correct" that means "NO". Your next question is to ask the "potential customer", "ARE WE THROUGH"? If the "potential customer" says, "YES", then respond

"I AM GLAD THAT YOU MADE THAT DECISION BECAUSE IT ELIMINATES THE DESIRE FOR ME TO "Chase" YOU."

At that time you will both have an understanding of the situation. The tension has been being released. Thank them and leave.

Look at Your Situation- I know what you are thinking. My list is dwindling and I am getting nowhere. Actually, you are fine tuning your sales technique. Now you could "brush aside" those "non-decision" potentials and search to find and work with those individuals that would use your services. I initially found it difficult to even think this way, but after the first experience you don't even realize the "power" that you control. It really gets easy. It makes the other person think differently toward you.

The Next Topic will discuss the half-truth considered Lies. By listening to only one side of a discussion without evaluating other options or expressions can cause you disastrous results

The "Half-Truth"

There are a lot of "half-truths" that are extremely dangerous and consequently lies. A common half-truth is that <u>as you get older, your saving style should be more conservative.</u> The "real truth" is <u>you should be more conservative with your savings only if your portfolio is "calculated" to be large enough to last the rest of your life.</u>

If you start saving when you are young, your period for accumulating money is longer, and your savings have more years to compound.

An example of the male age 25 with a cash value life insurance policy of $1,000,000? At age 65, his death benefit would be about $1,926,991; and he would be eligible to borrow about $750,000. At age 75, his death benefit would be about $3,101,916; and he would be eligible to borrow about $1,800,000.

Obviously, the longer you wait before you begin saving, the shorter the time you have available for accruing monies and allowing those monies to compound. <u>The worse risk would be – running out of money and you're still alive.</u>

Some of the information you see on televisions would be considered half-truths and extremely dangerous. Start doing research on everything you hear to determine if the information is truthful. There are so many newspapers from this country and other countries that may give you different offsetting opinions allowing you different paths to follow. By opening up your mind to different ideas you then have the capability for more open discussions.

The Next Topic will discuss a short history talking about the sliding down of the economy and the moving of the middle class toward the poverty level caused by outsourcing.

A Short History

Starting from the late 1800's, the majority of people coming to the United States had to make adjustments to living in a new society.

It was traditional for many to run their own family business and to encourage their children to follow their footsteps. Those who were living in the rural areas had the responsibility of making a living, producing food, providing shelter for their families and saving for emergencies. They were constantly busy, trying to make enough to survive.

With the start of the Industrial Revolution, many were encouraged to move from the rural areas of America to the cities by companies promising jobs, good pay, and a chance to advance, and above all, respect from the employer toward the employees. This seemed easier than the constant fight for survival.

Industrial unions were started for the purpose of establishing better wages, better working conditions, health care, and job security; instead of having to go it alone, the employee now had a union that would stand behind him to protect his rights.

While at first businesses offered a better way of life, over time they started to erode individual self-expression, family cohesiveness, and the ability to solve business and financial problems. The businesses started telling their employees how much they will be paid, when they can go on vacation, what kind of work they will perform, where they will work, and when they will work.

The decision-making progress was now in the hands of another. People were quick to learn that if they wanted to get ahead, it was best not to question the politics or policies of the company management.

After the Second World War- A lot of the new ideas that had been developed during the war was the impetus for new jobs during peacetime. Opportunities in the United States abounded. Transportation systems increased production of goods and services. Housing was affordable and jobs were plentiful.

With technological advancement came all the toys-- TV's PC's, etc. With new toys came a need to create a means to pay for the toys—and so came the credit card with the birth of the concept of "buy now, pay later." With credit cards came more spending, and more spending meant ultimately less saving.

With the advent of the credit card, even more toys proliferated-- modems, the internet, cell phones, electronic devices, and other convenient products. A more technologically advanced "comfortable lifestyle" changed us from savers into buyers.

Those born from 1946 through 1964 are the "baby boomers," and it is the same with generations that have come since. Their idea of living is that of the "buyers' market." Their wealth is in the collection of "stuff" and a "high style" of living.

Over the years working conditions and employer benefits started to improve. Among them was company saving accounts. Many employees started to contribute to these plans, making them feel like an integral part of the company. Employers began treating their employees with respect, offering them job security.

Companies against employees- As new production methods were being developed that removed the human element, many companies started to downsize. Loyalties that were once shared between the employer and employees began to vanish. These companies started to break the unions that had helped employees secure good wages, medical plans and decent working conditions.

In the 1990's, outsourcing was commonplace, leading to a reduction or even a shutdown of many businesses in the United States. Many employees were released from their jobs; and consequently, savings were lost. The focus for companies shifted now. Their biggest concern became their bottom line, their profit margin-- which unfortunately conflicted somewhat with providing for the needs of their employees.

What to do- In order to succeed, you have to be proactive and take charge of situations when they occur. Success depends on not procrastinating.

The Next Topic will discuss The Money Tracking Machine. Many people buy IRA's, 401K, 403B, stock, or mutual funds. Many have been turned off by what they hear on TV or radio. They get confused and do nothing. I will instruct you with the simplest ideas to grow your portfolio that has been tested using 18 different securities. I use the system daily for my own portfolio.

Chapter 12- How to Protect Stock and Mutual Funds from Loss

The Money Tracking System

This idea of tracking money will give ideas used by money managers in protecting their client's portfolios. <u>You will have the knowledge to do it yourself.</u>

I first started writing this information knowing that many people were <u>*"turned off"*</u> about protecting their retirement plans, stock or mutual funds because they listen to the radio or watched TV and were confused. The terminology was too complex, or they had little time to protect their money from loss.

I wrote this information for an 8th grader as having an assignment to buy a stock from a company they know. The technique to handle your retirement plans, stock or mutual funds is *easy to understand*. <u>It should take you about 20 seconds a day to keep tabs on your money.</u> If changes occur that are necessary to do something, such as calling the plan manager or financial consultant or broker to sell, buy or move the funds, plan to spend another ten minutes for the phone calls.

Is the amount of time tracking your retirement money each month worth saving thousands of dollars?

Once you learn how easy it is to track your money, teach your children.

For Mutual Funds or Stock- Most saving and retirement plans 401K, 403B, IRA's, variable annuities, and variable life insurance use the security market and rely on the use of mutual funds, stock, bonds, money market and other securities as the underlying process for producing future profits.

Unfortunately, the process of automatically controlling the loss of your premium and future profit, provided by life insurance companies for fixed annuities and fixed life insurance, is not available for other savings or retirement plans such as, stock, mutual funds, variable annuities, variable life insurance, 401K Plans, 403B Plans, Simple IRA's, Sep IRA's, Traditional or ROTH IRA's, and bond funds.

I suggest you follow this money tracking system that will allow you better control of your savings or retirement plan. Don't rely on your broker, or retirement plan manager, if you use one, to safeguard your funds.

Recently I spent time talking to the managers at Merrill Lynch, Smith Barney, UBS, Paine Webber, and even the large banks and found they do not have time tracking to protect your money from loss. Their job is to sell stock, bonds, mutual funds, life insurance, annuities, etc.

If your portfolio is near $500,000 managers will pursue the option of tracking, watching and controlling the buying and selling of your portfolio for a fee.

The Evaluation Process- The first process before you purchase stock or mutual funds is to evaluate the statistical information or the flow of money of the company's sales or services. It is necessary to understand the key statistics of a business.

This information can be found by using *YAHOO*. Open the *FINANCE* tag and key in the *SYMBOL* for the quote. An example- *DIS* for Disney. If you don't know the symbol you can find the symbol by supplying the company name that reviles the company information and symbol. (Please note- symbols will appear only on public companies.) When the quote is shown, on the left side of the screen is a tag marked *STATISTICS*. Open this tag. Most of the information you need can be found here.

Simply ask the following questions if you want to buy a stock: Is it a company you know? Is the company profitable? Is the company's revenue greater than the total debt? Does the company's quarterly return beat last year's quarterly returns?

That is what analysts look at- Does the company offer a dividend? If so, it is a great option. Is the company a leader in that particular industry? Is the stock price greater than $5.00? If the price is too low, the higher the risk. Keep away from the penny stocks. Is the number of shares traded daily high enough so that if you decide to sell, the trade can be done quickly.

Simply ask the following questions if you want to buy a mutual fund: Why do you want to buy mutual funds - long-term growth, high current income, or stability of principal? Depending on its objective, a fund may invest in stocks, bonds, cash investments, or a combination of these financial assets.

For Stock or Mutual Funds- you might look at the charts and use the maximum option to evaluate the flow of money over the years. This might be perfect for investing if the flow looks positive over a long period of time (moving upward from left to right).

The analysts determine and project in a report the changes of a stock usually determined by five categories. These categories are: Strong buy, Buy, Hold, Sell or Strong Sell. They may be called differently by different analysts, but the meaning is the same. Change in category usually affects the price of the stock either upward or downward.

Prior to publicizing the analyst's report, most purchases create an increase of the stock price. Usually if the report is positive, meeting the analyst's expectations or beating the analysts' expectations in a positive manner, the stock price could increase.

On occasion, if the stock price exceeds expectation more than expected, the prices may fall. This may seem illogical. The questions usually asked by the purchaser would be, the company did a tremendous job in sales this quarter- but are they able to do the same next quarter, probably not?

The biggest time of <u>caution</u> comes just before the analyst's report. If the analyst's reports are <u>unfavorable</u>, or <u>perceived to be unfavorable</u>, you should expect a reduction in the stock price. (Depending upon the analyst report, you should watch your stock to determine if action should be taken quickly.)

<u>The news found in quotes usually causes the stock prices to drop. If a company purchases another company, the purchasing company's stock prices will usually drop for fear of addition debt taken by the purchaser.</u>

A stock I bought in March 2009 was The Great Atlantic and Pacific Tea Company known as The A&P stores. The chart showed a trend that every time the security market fell the stock prices fell, and when the market changed upward, the prices rose. The company has been around since the late 1800's. They came through many down markets.

I decided to purchase it at $3.78 per share. The security went as high as $13.00 and fell to a low of $2.75. In December 2010 the company was bankrupt. That is why you should be cautious when buying stock from the pink sheet or lower than $5.00. The object is not to love your stock- but to use your stock to make money. I sold right after it hit the high. Now let's start into the ideas of tracking your money to prevent loss.

How to Determine the Buying Price- Volatility is simply the variation of the price of a stock or mutual fund from day to day or even month to month or year to year. A common way to calculate it is to take the standard deviation of the last 20 days (approximately one month of market days).

A simple way of calculating RISK --Go to Yahoo, Finance, and Historical. Find the *five* most current days of trade. Subtract from each date the <u>low of the day</u> from the <u>high of the day</u>. Accumulate a <u>total for the five</u> dates. Divide the accumulated number by 5 (five) giving an average daily RISK. This gives you the average for 1 day of trade, what I consider an average RISK.

In this time period of high volatility in the security market, I suggest using from 2 to 2 1/2 days of RISK for buying your stock or mutual fund.

How to Determine When to Sell- I usually use a percent to determine how much off the top price if you decide to SELL.

Examples: (for buying I will use $.54 as a *one day RISK* -- 2.5 times $.54 = $1.35 -- selling – 3.5 %.)

Twice each month you should recalculate the average daily RISK by using the method shown above. If the average daily RISK starts to <u>increase</u> use a higher percentage for calculating the SELL option. If the average daily RISK starts to <u>decrease</u> use a lower percentage for calculating the SELL option.

How to BUY Securities When Prices Drop- <u>(Use paper trading - you are not buying- just keeping a list)</u> as the prices move downward. <u>Add</u> the <u>closed price</u> to (the RISK). That is now your proposed buy option.

Example: closed price was $12.87- buy at approximately $12.87 + $1.35 = $14.22.

The prices are still dropping: Example: closed price was $12.44- buy at approximately $12.44 + $1.35 = $13.79.

The prices are still dropping: Example: closed price was $11.99- buy at approximately $11.99 + $1.35 = $13.34.

The prices are starting to rise - For the buy option -- if the prices hit the $13.34 or above that, BUY the security.

If you were *paper trading* (by tracking the buying and selling of stock or mutual funds without risking any money.) By pretending and following a stock or mutual fund as the prices fall, you are fortunate to get in at the beginning. I did that with Disney and General Electric.

The question comes up as to why use a couple of days RISK as the buying option? *The answer is to bypass the thrashing of the stock or mutual fund price and to firm up a good potential place and dollar amount when buying.*

The RISK of the price falling could occur until the stock or mutual fund price moves upward to what you feel is a comfortable position. The tracking process should continue.

Another way to Buy Securities when Prices Drop- And *it requires a lot more caution,* and has some disadvantages, would be at the end of each trading day recalculate the five day risk price. Use a one (1) risk day <u>subtracted</u> from the closed price. If you are using an online trading system use the *trade tag* and enter the *Symbol*, *BUY* option, *Quantity*, and the results of your subtraction for buying using the *Limit* option. Execute the order for the next day's trade. As an example you had $10,000 to buy shares minus $10.00 for the transaction cost. You would divide $9,990 by $36.43 and get about 274 shares.

Example: close price = $37.42 and the risk price = $.99. The *Limit* would be $37.42 - $.99 or $36.43. Example of the order: *Symbol* WYN, *Option* BUY, *Shares* 274, *Limit Order* $36.43.

If the stock low price hits $36.43 or lower, the shares are bought and the advantage would be purchasing more shares at a low price. If you were to buy stock with the other option (above) you would have fewer shares. The *disadvantage of this option* would be the stock prices drop again the following days. *If closing prices start to rise, quit this option and use the first option above.* If the stock was not bought, repeat this option again.

How to BUY Stock or Mutual Funds if Prices are Rising‑ Look in the historical tab and use the prior days closed price for stock and the NAV price for mutual funds as your starting point. Make that the bottom price for the security and then follow the example as shown above.

High	Low	Difference	Close Price
35.59	34.41	$1.18	35.51
35.12	34.12	$1.00	*34.86*
34.71	33.36	$1.35	34.52
34.43	33.78	$0.65	34.01
35.18	34.26	$0.92	34.30

$5.10 / 5 = average $1.02.

1.25 times $1.02 = $1.28 as the buy option – if the prices hit the $34.86 + $1.28 = $36.14 or above that, BUY the stock or mutual fund.

This security is Checkpoint Software—symbol CHKP. The above dates are from September 22, 2010 through September 28, 2010. As of October 7, 2010 the closing price was $37.75. If you bought the stock on October 15, 2008 the closing price was $17.43. Evaluate the statistics for this company and see why I bought this stock.

How to SELL stock or mutual fund if prices start to Drop- I will use as an example 3.5% percent. Multiply the closed price for stock or NAV price for mutual funds by (.035). Subtract that total from the closed price or NAV price. That is now your proposed SELL option.

Example: price was $22.87- sell at $22.87 - $.80 = $22.07.

The prices are starting to fall- Example: The price is $22.61- This price is higher than the selling price or NAV price of $22.07-- therefore no action should be taken to sell. The prices are still rising: Example: price was $23.01-recalculate a new SELL at $23.01 - $.81 = $22.20.

The prices are dropping- Example: price is now $22.18. This drop in price is lower than the closed price or NAV price of $22.20-- SELL NOW. If you still like the stock or mutual fund, paper trade the prices as they start to drop and buy it again.

How to determine Gain verses Loss as a Percentage- The calculation for Gain verses Loss starts with the buy option plus the average cost per share when you buy and sell a stock or mutual fund.

This is the transaction fee for buying and selling only example- If you bought 100 shares of a stock or mutual fund at a cost of a $10.00 transaction fee, and later sold the 100 shares at the same transaction fee, the transaction cost per share is $.20. The Gain verses Loss should be calculated at $10 + the transaction fee of $.20.

The Calculation for Gain Verses Loss as an example- Cost price per Share including buy cost and sell cost + stock price is $10.20. If the next day's close price is $10.87.

The formula is the days Closed Price (-) Cost Price per Share = difference. Difference / Cost Price per Share = value that should be calculated as a percent.

In this example it is $10.87- $10.20 =.67.--.67/$10.20 = .0657 times 100 gives 6.57% gain.

If the following day's close price is $9.87- The formula is Closed Price - Cost Price per Share = difference. Difference / Cost Price per Share = value that should be calculated as a percent.

In this example it is $9.87- $10.20 = -.33. ----.33/$10.20 = -.0324 times 100 gives (-3.24)% loss.

How to Determine the Selling Price- the Selling Price is a calculation used when the stock or mutual fund reaches a high price and then starts to fall. This is a scale, as the high price can be reached at different times. You are trying to avoid selling too early in case the prices start to rise.

Example: The high price is reached at $15.67 and start to fall. In this *example* I am using a 3.5% off the high price. *You use what is comfortable for you*. If the stock or mutual fund is very volatile, you may want to use different percentages for the high selling price.

In the example: $15.65 * .035 = $.547 rounded upward to $.55. $15.65 – $.55 = $15.15. When the price drops equal to or lower than the $15.15 selling price, the stock or mutual fund is sold.

The idea is to not fall in love with the stock or mutual fund you own. The old method of buy and hold forever is gone. The new idea is "Get in, Get up, and get off quickly." *Successful tracking* of your money is the start of money managing.

You have to take charge of your own savings or retirement plans. To be successful tracking your money, start with the following information:

Before buying any stock or mutual fund, check Yahoo finance, check for the stock or mutual fund you want to evaluate, look at the statistics, charts, and latest news information about the stock or mutual fund to determine if it meets your risk level.

If you plan to buy stock or mutual funds appearing to be on a downward path, don't buy the stock or mutual fund now, but use the Trailing-Down-of-Price routine, "paper-trading," waiting for the buy signal when the stock or mutual fund finally bottoms and starts to rise.

If you own the stock or mutual fund, <u>follow the process for tracking as the prices rise or fall.</u>

Check with your financial consultant or retirement plan coordinator to let them know that you are tracking your stock or mutual fund and will notify them when to move the money to the money market when prices start to drop, or to buy the stock or mutual fund when you receive a buy signal.

If you "day trade" the money tracking system offers more flexibility and would generate greater results.

Calculating your profit is easy. You start with the purchase price of the stock or mutual fund subtracted from the selling price giving a profit dollar. The selling price is then divided into the profit dollar times 100 giving a profit percent.

Rule 72- *__Keep away from greed and succeed__*.
The following information is necessary for you to
understand why you should protect your money. <u>Divide
the percentage you think the stock or mutual fund will
achieve into 72.</u> That is the number of years you need to
double your money.

There have been about 28 down markets since the
1930's, occurring about every 6 years. The money lost
over those years could have been saved if the money
tracking system was used. You would need to average
12% yearly just to break even from down markets.

Later you will see examples of Checkpoint
Software, IBM, and Disney of what happens if you don't
protect your money from loss. Please note: they did not
average 12% over 14 years.

Don't procrastinate. Don't fall in love with your
stock or mutual fund when prices drop. Follow the rules
of the money tracking system exactly to be successful in
protecting your money from loss.

Success Verses Loss- When you receive
information from The Money Tracking Machine
software to do something with your money, it shouldn't
take you more than <u>a few minutes</u> to contact your broker
or plan manager.

If you wait and your money is lost, even with an 8
% return, doubling your money takes <u>9 years</u>. In fact,

within those 9 years, there occurred, on average, <u>a down market every 6 years</u>. Lots of luck getting your money to what it was before the loss. What would you rather have, a few minutes of tracking your money from loss, or years trying to recoup your money?

If you do not have a computer or do not know how to operate a computer, or don't want to be bothered by the time involved to manage and protect your securities, *I will*. I will use the money tracking software I created to protect your stock or mutual funds. Please call for more information.

Stock/ Mutual Fund -- Purchases- I suggest not purchasing a stock or mutual fund with a price equal to or less than $5.00 per share or stock sold on the "pink sheet." The price may be cheap, but <u>the risk level is high</u>. The sales are usually low, and when you decide to sell, you may find it difficult finding a buyer when prices are dropping.

The money tracking system works in *every* market condition. When stock or mutual fund prices are falling, you should do *"paper trading"* (tracking on paper) waiting for the time to buy.

IRAS, 401K, 403B plans, Variable & Fixed Accounts- These funds are privately held, created, or are standard mutual funds found in the market. The fund managers should supply the <u>symbol</u> of the security and the <u>name of the fund</u>. They may have an equivalent fund similar to the one being used in the mutual fund market. If their funds don't have a symbol or fund name found in the marketplace, ask for the web site where the daily NAV price can be obtained.

Evaluating your Stock or Mutual Funds- An easy way of evaluating your stock or mutual funds is to use the Internet. Startup Yahoo and then enter the <u>finance section.</u> *For stock only*- Enter the stock symbol or the name of the company to find the security <u>symbol</u>. *For mutual funds only*- Under the <u>investing tag</u>, select <u>mutual funds</u>. You can find the funds by name.

Once you reach the screen "Get Quotes Results for" (your funds,) under exchange, look for NAS (NASDAQ.) Once you find the fund name and symbol, select <u>symbol.</u>

For Mutual Funds or Stock- Once you find the price of the stock or mutual funds, use their <u>basic</u> or <u>interactive chart</u> as an evaluating tool. These charts offer many features. You can choose a range of dates and time to evaluate the open, high, low, close or NAV for mutual funds of many trading periods.

By observing multiple time periods you now can determine if the stock or mutual fund prices are currently rising or falling. This is useful in determining what stock or mutual fund you wish to buy now or to *"paper trade"* for future buying.

There is a <u>historical tag</u> that provides historical prices offering many date ranges. <u>This will be used to initially gather the volatility of each stock or mutual fund.</u>

For Stock Only- Use the five (5) most current dates. Find the total differences of <u>the high and low price.</u>

Example:

Jan 02 high $75.25 low $74.25 difference $1.00
Jan 03 high $74.95 low $72.85 difference $2.10
Jan 04 high $73.50 low $72.25 difference $1.25
Jan 05 high $74.50 low $72.50 difference $2.00
Jan 06 high $72.75 low $71.55 difference $1.20.

Total differences $7.55 divided by 5 = $1.51. Use $1.51 as the 1 day RISK. Every stock has a RISK level. By evaluating these differences you get the RISK of the security.

Getting Started- You will be using the <u>closed</u> price (called NAV for mutual funds) in the <u>historical</u> section calculated at the end of day processing.

The high and low price of mutual funds is <u>not an option</u> and <u>should not be used</u> to determine future RISK of all mutual funds.

Getting Volatility of Mutual Funds- uses the six (6) most current closed prices and determines the total differences of <u>the closed price</u>. Divide this total by 5.

Example:

Jan 02 close 75.20 Jan 03 close 73.00 difference $2.20
Jan 03 close 74.95 Jan 04 close 72.85 difference $2.10
Jan 04 close 73.50 Jan 05 close 72.50 difference $1.00
Jan 05 close 74.50 Jan 06 close 71.50 difference $3.00
Jan 06 close 72.75 Jan 07 close 71.55 difference $1.20.

Total differences $9.50 divided by 5 = $1.90.

About twice each month you should recalculate the RISK for mutual funds by using the above method. Keep a daily record of the closed prices or NAV for mutual funds and the transaction date. Now use the same method for calculating the buying and selling as shown before.

Take Charge of Your Stock or Mutual fund- Now that you know what to do, call the plan managers or financial consultant to <u>move your money to the money market when prices are starting to fall,</u> or take your money <u>from the money market to buy stock or mutual funds when prices are starting to rise</u>. Now you can *<u>buy</u>*

more shares from the saved money to increase your portfolio.

    Why protect your stock or mutual fund from loss- With an average down market every 6 years, and by using rule 72, you would need to average *12%,* just to break even on your savings. Your savings would take 6 years for your money to double. This could happen if you did not use the money tracking system.

    In evaluating what happened in the past – Check Point Software Technology CHKP will be calculated for 14 years for the return on an investment.

    The following is what happened if you bought *195 shares* of CHKP at $22.00 per share spending *$4,290* in January 1997 and held the security and _didn't use the money tracking system_ to protect your investment from loss. (The 2010 ending date is the 22nd of November.)

The buy and hold forever method.

Year	Jan $$	Dec $$	YTD%	YTD$
1997	$21.37	$40.75	90.69%	$7,946.25
1998	$40.50	$40.13	(.09%)	$7,825.35
1999	$43.19	$97.53	125.82%	$19,018.35
2000	$109.25	*$133.56*	22.25%	*$26,044.20*
2001	$110.50	$39.89	(177.01%)	$7,778.35
2002	$40.69	$13.05	(69.98%)	$2,544.75
2003	*$14.69*	$17.00	15.72%	$3,315.00

2004	$18.84	$24.47	29.68%	$4,771.65
2005	*$24.85*	$20.06	(19.28%)	$3,991.70
2006	$20.42	$21.92	7.35%	$4,274.40
2007	$22.58	$22.26	(1.42%)	$4,340.70
2008	$21.87	$18.96	(13.31%)	$3,697.20
2009	$19.94	$34.27	78.67%	$6,682.65
2010	$34.11	$43.82	28.47%	$8,544.90

The return calculated from *$8,544.90* and *$4,290* is *99.19 %*, and a *14 year* average return of *7.09%*.

The Money Tracking System- By using the money tracking system in January 2001 your *$24,620 for 195 shares* was moved to the money market or sold.

In 2003 you used $24,620 and bought *1640 shares* at $15 per share. In 2005 your *$36,080* for 1640 shares at *$22* per share was moved to the money market or sold. In 2009 you used *$36,080* and bought *1718* shares at $21 per share. By November 22, 2010 the value per share was $43.82 with a profit of *$75,282.76.*

The return calculated from $75,282.76 and $8,544.90 was 781.03% with a 14 year return of 55.79%. The return calculated from $75,282.76 and $4,290 was 1654.84% with a 14 year return of 118.20%. What would you rather have *$8,544.90* or *$75,282.76?*

*Buying at the Top-*What would happen if you purchased *CHKP –* Checkpoint Software Company near the top price of $130.00 per share in the year 2000?

Year	Jan $$	Dec $$	YTD%	YTD$
2000	$109.25	*$133.56*	22.25%	*$26,044.20*
2001	$110.50	$39.89	(177.01%)	$7,778.35
2002	$40.69	$13.05	(69.98%)	$2,544.75
2003	*$14.69*	$17.00	15.72%	$3,315.00
2004	$18.84	$24.47	29.68%	$4,771.65
2005	*$24.85*	$20.06	(19.28%)	$3,991.70
2006	$20.42	$21.92	7.35%	$4,274.40
2007	$22.58	$22.26	(1.42%)	$4,340.70
2008	$21.87	$18.96	(13.31%)	$3,697.20
2009	$19.94	$34.27	78.67%	$6,682.65
2010	$34.11	$43.82	28.47%	$8,544.90

$130.00 per share times 195 shares = $25,350. In 2001 you moved your 195 shapes at a price of $110.00 or $21,450 to the money market or sold. *Please note the loss.* In 2003 you used your $21,450 and bought 1430 shares at $15.00 per share. In 2005 you moved your 1430 shares at a price of $22.00 or $31,430 to the money market or sold. In 2009 you use your $31,430 and bought 1498 shares at $21.00 per share. By December 31, 2010 the share price was $46.26 and the 1498 shares had a value of $69,297.48.

The return over the 11 years was 173.36% averaging 15.67% yearly. *By tracking your money, recouping your money is possible.*

The Walt Disney Company- In evaluating what happened in the past Walt Disney Company DIS will be calculated for 14 years for the return on an investment. If you bought *100 shares* in January 1997 at $69.00 per share and held the stock and *didn't use the money tracking system* to protect your investment from loss. (The 2010 ending date is the 22nd of November.)

Buy and hold forever method.

Year	Jan $$	Dec $$	YTD%	YTD$
1997	$67.37	$99.00	46.95%	$9,900
1998	$99.62	$29.87	(70.02%)	$2,987
1999	$29.56	$29.12	(1.49%)	$2,912
2000	$29.25	$28.94	(1.06%)	$2,894
2001	$27.94	$20.95	(25.02%)	$2,095
2002	$21.45	$16.04	(33.73%)	$1,604
2003	$17.26	$23.30	34.99%	$2,330
2004	$23.67	$27.88	17.79%	$2,788
2005	$27.80	$23.07	(13.78%)	$2,307
2006	$24.40	$34.27	40.45%	$3,427
2007	$34.20	$32.42	(5.20%)	$3,242
2008	$31.77	$22.48	(29.24%)	$2,248
2009	$23.92	$32.28	34.94%	$3,228
2010	$32.09	$36.95	15.22%	$3,695

The return calculated from $3,695 and $6,900 was *(46.45%)*, with a *14 year* average return of *(3.32%.)*

By using the money tracking system in January 1998 your *$9,650 for your 100 shares* was moved to the money market or sold. In 2003 you used *$9,650* and bought 640 *shares* at $15 per share. In 2005 your *$16,000 for* 640 shares at *$25* per share was moved to the money market or sold. In 2006 you used *$16,000* and bought 666 *shares* at $24 per share. In 2007 your *$21,978 for 666 shares* at *$33* per share was moved to the money market or sold. By 2009 you bought *955* shares at $23 per share. By November 22, 2010 the value per share was $36.95 with a profit of *$35,287.25*.

The return is calculated from $35,287.25 and $3,695 was 855% with a 14 year return of 61.07%. The return is calculated from $35,287.25 and $6,900 was 411.41% with a 14 year return of 29.39%. What would you rather have *$3,695* or *$35,287.25?*

The Federal Realty Investment Trust- In evaluating what happened in the past Federal Realty Investment Trust FRT will be calculated for 11 years for the return on an investment. The following is what would happen if you bought *100 shares* of FRT in January 2000 at $19 per share and held the stock and *didn't use the money tracking system* to protect your investment from loss. (The 2010 ending date is the 22nd of November.)

The buy and hold forever method.

Year	Jan $$	Dec $$	YTD%	YTD$
2000	$18.81	$19.00	(1.01%)	$1,900
2001	$19.06	$23.16	21.51%	$2,316
2002	$22.93	$28.05	22.33%	$2,815
2003	$28.35	$39.13	38.02%	$3,913
2004	$38.55	$52.24	35.51%	$5,224
2005	$51.65	$60.65	17.42%	$6,065
2006	$61.63	$85.00	37.92%	$8,500
2007	$84.46	$81.15	(3.92%)	$8,115
2008	$78.87	$59.24	(24.89%)	$5,924
2009	$59.42	$69.50	16.96%	$6,950
2010	$67.03	$78.86	17.65%	$7,886

The return calculated from *$7,886* and *$1,900* was 315.05%, with an *11 year* average return of 28.64%.

By using the money tracking system in 2007 your *$8,200* for 100 shares at *$82* per share was moved to the money market or sold. In 2009 you used $8,200 and bought *132 shares* at *$62* per share. By November 22, 2010 the value per share was *$78.86* with a profit of *$10,409.52*. The return calculated for $10,409.52 and the $7.886 was 32%. The 11 year average return was 2.19%. The return calculated for $10,409.52 and the $1,900 was 447.87%. The 11 year average return was 40.72%. What would you rather have $7,886 or $10,409.52?

International Business Machines Corporation IBM

- In evaluating what happened in the past International Business machines Corporation IBM will be calculated for 13 years for the return on an investment. The following is what would happen if you bought *100 shares* of IBM in January 1998 at *$105.62* per share and held the security and *didn't use the money tracking system* to protect your investment from loss. (The 2010 ending date is the 22nd of November.)

The buy and hold forever method.

Year	Jan $$	Dec $$	YTD%	YTD$
1998	$105.62	$186.75	76.81%	$18,675
1999	$183.00	$108.75	(40.57%)	$10,875
2000	$116.06	$85.00	(26.76%)	$8,500
2001	$94.62	$122.90	29.89%	$12,290
2002	$123.66	$76.26	(38.34%)	$7,626
2003	$81.65	$92.63	13.45%	$9.263
2004	$91.55	$98.30	7.37%	$9,830
2005	$97.75	$82.20	(15.91%)	$8,220
2006	$82.06	$97.15	18.39%	$9,715
2007	$97.27	$110.09	13.18%	$11,009
2008	$104.90	$83.55	(20.35%)	$8,355
2009	$87.37	$132.57	51.73%	$13,257
2010	$132.45	$145.39	9.77%	$14,539

The return calculated from $14,539 and $105.62 was 37.65% with a 13 year average return of 2.90%.

Using the money tracking system in January 1999 your *$17,500* for *100 shares* was *moved* to the money market or sold. In 2001 you used *$17,500* and bought *176* shares at *$99* per share. In 2002 your *$20,064* for *176* shares at *$114* per share was moved to the money market or sold. In 2003 you used *$20,064* and bought *264* shares at *$76* per share. In 2008 your *$25,872* for *264* shares at *$98* per share was moved to the money market or sold. In 2009 you use *$25,842* to buy *284* shares at *$91* per share. By November 22, 2010 the value per share was $ *145.39* with a profit of *$41,290.76*. The return calculated from $41,290.76 and $14,539 was 184% with a 13 year average return of 14.15%. The return calculated from $41,290.76 and $10,562 was 290.94% with a 13 year average return of 22.38%. What would you rather have *$41,209.76 or $14,539.*

Dollar cost averaging- Let's assume you could afford $100 every month to buy *Disney shares*. The best way would be to add dollars monthly. The above chart for Disney is by the year. $1,200 was moved to the money market or sold at the beginning of each year. The share price was divided into $1,200. Fractional shares would not be used. In 1998, 1999, 2000, 2001, 2002 and 2003 you added $7,200 to your $9,650 or $16,850 was moved to the money market. In 2003 you used $16,850 and bought *1123* shares at $15 per share. In 2004 you used $1,200 and bought *49* shares at $25 per share to increase the shares to *1172*. In 2005 your $29,300 at $25 per share plus $1,200 equal to $30,500 was moved to the money market. In 2006 you used $30,500 plus $1,200 or $31,700 and bought *1320* at $24 per share. In 2007 your $43,560 plus $1,200 equal to $44,760 at $33 per share was moved to the money market. In 2008 you added $1,200 plus $44,750 equal to $45,950 was moved to the money market. In 2009 you added $1,200 plus $45,950 equal to $47,150 and bought *2050* shares at $23 per share. In 2010 you used $1,200 and bought 36 shares at $33 per share increasing your shares to 2086. Over the 14 years you used $16,800 at $1,200 per year to increase your portfolio. By November 22, 2010 the value per share was *$36.95 with a profit of* $76,973.40.

The key to wealth is to <u>buy more shares</u> with money you saved when prices are dropping and to compound your savings by adding money monthly.

Without managing and protecting your savings, the following occurred- In the year 2000 the Standard and Poor's 500 was $1441 and two years later dropped to $800. $1441 minus $800 equal $641 per share lost in two years or a 46% drop in savings.

If you had $100,000 in the year 2000 and <u>didn't protect</u> your securities from loss, the value in 2002 would have been about $55,000. By using "The Money Tracking System" to save your money, the loss was limited to about $107.57.

"The money tracking system" offers a more practical objective way of limiting your share loss by having your extra savings in the money market. Later, you could have purchased more shares when the market hit the low of $800 and started to rise.

By allowing the share price to drop and your savings now worth $55,000 *you lost four ways*. Not having the necessary money in the future to maintain your lifestyle with the possibility of "running out of money and your still alive. "The silent thief—inflation; being taxable; compounding; and is eroding your buying power of future necessities.

There have been 28 downward type markets in the past since the 1930. *This downward situation seems to occur every six years.* By neglecting future downward markets you are putting your savings and retirement plans in an unstable condition.

You read about rule 72, or the time it takes for your money to double. When you are young, you may have time to recoup your loss. From age 55 and beyond, the risk of money loss is the biggest issue. The rule is very simply dividing the percentage you figure you can achieve, over a long period of time, into 72.

Example: 8% earnings would take 9 years.

If your loss went from $100,000 to $50,000, you would have your original $100,000 by age 64. What really occurred was out of your control. By the end of 2008 there was a large downturn in the market falling about 50% within a three week period. If you used the above method for determining falling markets, your money would have been saved.

The Next Topic will discuss inflation the silent thief. Saving plans must beat the cost of inflation. Being too conservative may be detrimental as a saving idea because of loss of future buying options.

Chapter 13 - Inflation the Silent Thief

What is inflation-

Inflation (the cost of living) compounds and is taxable? The best example would be: A cup of coffee this year will cost you $1.00 (+) tax; next year, $1.04 (+) tax; and $1.09 (+) tax in two years.

The following is a system that allows you to compute the expense of inflation. Use the computed amount to calculate how much extra money you need to save over the years-- just to keep up your lifestyle. The same system will calculate the eroding buying power of your savings from year-to-year. The formula will adjust to the different tax brackets. Most financial consultants use an average of 4 percent as the standard inflation rate, without including the added-on tax.

The Break-Even Factor- The break-even against inflation includes the tax and is calculated for every tax bracket, increasing as taxes increase for every tax brackets.

For the *10* percent tax bracket, the break-even-percentage against inflation is 4.29 percent.

For the *15* percent tax bracket, the break-even-percentage against inflation is 4.60 percent.

For the *25* percent tax bracket, the break-even percentage against inflation is 5.13 percent.

For the *28* percent tax bracket, the break-even percentage against inflation is 5.80 percent.

For the *33* percent tax bracket, the break-even percentage against inflation is 6.67 percent.

For the *35* percent tax bracket, the break-even percentage against inflation is 7.84 percent.

Why is this Break-Even Against Inflation Necessary- As the cost of everything generally increases yearly, your savings must increase yearly just to have enough money to meet the rising cost of your new purchases. The formula above will calculate the new inflation expense and the eroded buying power of your saving.

Inflation Dollars – 10 Percent- This example will show the extra money that would be necessary over a two-year period to buy what $1,000 will buy this year.

Year one: $1,000 savings (x) .0429 = $42.90. You would need an additional $42.90 the first year-- or a total of $1,042.90. *Year two*: $1,042.90 savings (x) .0429 = $44.74 (+) $42.90. You would need an additional $87.64 the second year-- or a total of $1,087.64.

Money Erosion – 10 Percent Bracket- These examples will show how $1,000 would <u>erode over</u> a two-year period.

Year one: $1,000 (x) .0429 = $42.90. $1,000 (-) $42.90 = $957.10. Your $1,000 savings would erode by $42.90 the first year. *Year two*: $1,087.64 (x) .0429 = $46.66. $957.10 (-) $46.66 = $910.44. Your savings the second year-- would erode by a total of $89.56.

Inflation Dollars – 15 percent Bracket- these examples will show the extra money that would be necessary over a two-year period to buy what $1,000 will buy this year.

Year one: $1,000 savings (x) .0460 = $46.00. You would need an additional $46.00 the first year-- or a total of $1,046.00. *Year two*: $1,046.00 savings (x) .0460 = $48.12 (+) $46.00. You would need an additional $94.12 the second year-- or a total of $1,094.12.

Money Erosion – 15 Percent Bracket- These examples will show how $1,000 would <u>erode over</u> a two-year period.

Year one: $1,000 (x) .0460 = $46.00. $1,000 (-) $46.00 = $954.00. Your savings would erode by $46.00 the first year. *Year two*: $1,094.12 (x) .0460 = $50.33. $954.00 (-) $50.33 = $903.67. Your savings the second year-- would erode by a total of $96.33.

Inflation Dollars – 25 Percent-These examples will show the extra money that would be necessary over a two-year period to buy what $1,000 will buy this year.

Year one: $1,000 savings (x) .0513 = $51.30. You would need an additional $51.30 the first year-- or a total of 1,051.30. *Year two*: $1,051.30 savings (x) .0513 = $53.93 (+) $51.30. You would need an additional $105.23 the second year-- or a total $1,105.23.

Money Erosion – 25 Percent Bracket-These examples will show how money would <u>erode </u>over a two-year period.

Year one: $1,000 (x) .0513 = $51.30. $1,000 (-) $51.30 = $948.70. Your $1,000 savings would erode by $51.30 the first year. *Year two*: $1,105.23 (x) .0513 = $56.70. $948.70 (-) $56.70 = $894.77. Your savings the second year-- would erode by a total of $108.00.

Inflation Dollars – 28 Percent- These examples will show the extra money that would be necessary over a two-year period to buy what $1,000 will buy this year.

Year one: $1,000 savings (x) .0580 = $58.00.You would need an additional $58.00 the first year or a total of $1,058.00. *Year two*: $1,058.00 savings (x) .0580 = $61.36 (+) $58.00. You would need an additional $119.36 the second year-- or a total of $1,119.36.

Money Erosion – 28 Percent Bracket- These examples will show how money would erode over a two-year period.

Year one: $1,000 (x) .0580 = $58.00. $1,000 (-) $58.00 = $942.00. Your $1,000 savings would erode by $58.00 the first year. *Year two*: $1,119.36 (x) .0580 = $64.92. $942.00 (-) $64.92 = $877.08. Your savings the second year-- would erode by a total of $122.92.

Inflation Dollars – 33 Percent- These examples will show the extra money that would be necessary over a two-year period to buy what $1,000 will buy this year.

Year one: $1,000 savings (x) .0667 = $66.70. You would need an additional $66.70 the first year or a total $1,066.70. *Year two*: $1,066.70 savings (x) .0667 = $71.15 (+) $66.70. You would need an additional $137.85 the second year-- or a total of $1,137.85.

Money Erosion – 33 Percent Bracket- These examples will show how money would erode over a two-year period.

Year one: $1,000 (x) .0667 = $66.70. $1,000 (-) $66.70 = $933.30. Your $1,000 savings would erode by $66.70 the first year. *Year two*: starting at $1,137.85 (x) .0667 = $75.90. $933.30 (-) $75.90 = $857.40. Your savings the second year-- would erode by a total of $142.60.

Inflation Dollars - 35 Percent-These examples will show the extra money that would be necessary over a two-year period to buy what $1,000 will buy this year.

Year one: $1,000 savings (x) .0784 = $78.40. You would need an additional $78.40 the first year or a total of $1,078.40.*Year two*: $1,078.40 savings (x) .0784 = $84.55 (+) $78.40. You would need an additional $162.95 the second year-- or a total of $1,162.95.

Money Erosion – 35 Percent Bracket- These examples will show how money would erode over a two-year period.

Year one: $1,000 (x) .0784 = $78.40. $1,000 (-) 78.40 = $921.60. Your $1,000 savings would erode by $78.40 the first year. *Year two*: $1,162.95 (x) .0784 = $91.18. $921.60 (-) $91.18 = $830.42. Your savings the second year-- would erode by $169.58.

Eroded buying power- As you can see, no matter what tax bracket you're in, *taxes and inflation can erode your savings.* Therefore, it is necessary not only to increase your savings each year by an amount that will offset inflation you must--find the right vehicle by which your savings will have the opportunity to compound.

That is the reason I use-- and suggest you use-- mutual funds and stock to beat inflation. CD's, money market, bonds (taxable and tax-free) -- will not beat inflation over the years.

The Next Topic will discuss controlling the money. Wal-Mart the largest retail in the United States has been sued so many times due mainly to their actions toward other small competitive companies and against their unfair labor practices toward their employees. This case went to the Supreme Court who refused to bring it up. By not acting it was as if discrimination is still considered legal, and these practices of discrimination are being used by some of the governors and state assemblies personal to lower services and create unemployment for offsetting their states budgets. Many people are stepping up and petitioning against the governors and state assembly members. Discrimination in a way to changing voting laws, making it harder to vote, is starting to be challenged by many.

Chapter 14 -Controlling the Money By Discriminating

Discrimination in the workplace

This has been challenged quite a few times. Unequal pay among men and women for doing the same job is the issue of this supreme course case. This is a case of sex discrimination.

You are probably wondering why this issue is being brought up when discussing the monetary plan and the budget. If companies or corporations are allowed to discriminate, it affects the livelihood of individuals and opens the door to other discriminating ideas of lowering the standard of living for all workers. Some of the states have already created resolutions and passed bills to destroy unions and disallowing pension plans.

There are petitions being filled out by ordinary people in Wisconsin and Ohio to put on the ballot bills to be voted on to offset the discriminating laws that were passed by the legislators of those states. At present, petitions are being signed to remove the governor of Wisconsin.

The following class action suit started the process by the Supreme Court allowing discrimination.

US Supreme Court: Proving Commonality a Hurdle for Future Class Actions.

Sue M. Bendavid is chair of the Employment Law Department at Lewitt Hackman in Encino, California. Her department represents employers in employment law matters. For more information regarding her practice, go to www.lewitthackman.com.

On June 20, the U.S. Supreme Court issued a long-awaited opinion in the nation's largest ever sex discrimination case, ruling in favor of Wal-Mart Stores Inc. This decision is not only "big news" for Wal-Mart; it raises other significant issues for employers nationwide who have been named as defendants in class actions by their employees.

The lawsuit was brought on behalf of 1.5 million current and former female employees who worked for various Wal-Mart retail stores throughout the United States. The lead plaintiff, *(The party, who initiates a lawsuit,)* Betty Dukes initially worked as a cashier and later promoted to customer service manager. She was then demoted to cashier and greeter after she engaged in a series of disciplinary violations. Along with others she filed a sex discrimination class action arguing Wal-Mart violated Title VII of the Civil Rights Act of 1964. *(Title VII prohibits employment discrimination based on race, color, religion, sex and national origin.)*

She stated that after five years of working for Wal-Mart she was denied opportunities to train for a management position and was demoted after she complained. The others made similar allegations and claimed they too were denied advancement opportunities because of their sex.

In an effort to prove the case deserved class treatment, Betty Dukes and the others submitted statistical evidence about pay and promotion disparities, anecdotal reports (refers both to evidence that is factually unreliable, as well as evidence that may be true but cherry-picked or otherwise unrepresentative of typical cases and is considered untrustworthy.)

By approximately 120 employees and testimony of a sociologist, Dr. William Bielby, who analyzed Wal-Mart's culture and practices stating Wal-Mart was "vulnerable" to gender discrimination.

At the trial level, the U.S. District Court certified the class in 2004. The 9th U.S. Circuit Court of Appeals substantially affirmed the District Court's certification order concluding that Betty Dukes and the others had the right to- "raise the common question whether Wal-Mart's female employees nationwide were subjected to a single set of corporate policies (not merely a number of independent discriminatory acts) that may have worked to unlawfully discriminate against them in the violation of Title VII."

In strongly rejecting all of Betty Dukes and the others evidence, the U.S. Supreme Court reversed and held that a sharing of common ideas- (*whether a* class action *is superior to individual litigation depends on the case, and is determined by the judge's ruling on a motion for* class certification) – could not be established.

The Court's opinion centered on the issue of "commonality," (see the definition above,) and stated that Betty dukes and the others must demonstrate that "class members," (Betty dukes and the others), "have suffered the same injury" – not merely that they all suffered a violation of the same law.

The question is on the reasons [why] employees were treated the way they were, which, under the facts of this case, could not be determined on a class-wide basis.

"What matters to class certification...is not the raising of common 'questions' – even in droves – but, rather the amount of paperwork showing proof to establish a class wide proceeding to generate common [*answers] that are necessary to drive the resolution of the litigation..."

As the Court recognized, without lots of proof holding together the reasons for the various employee decisions that were made, the Court stated it would be impossible to say that all class members would produce a common answer to the crucial discrimination question of "why was I disfavored."

The Court noted that to prove commonality, Betty Dukes and the others would have needed to demonstrate-Wal-Mart used either a biased testing procedure or submit significant proof that Wal-Mart operated under a general policy of discrimination and that discrimination manifested itself in hiring and promotion practices in the same general fashion.

Betty dukes and the others could not meet this burden. In fact, the Court recognized that <u>Wal-Mart's announced policy prohibits sex discrimination.</u> Since local supervisors were given discretion over employee matters, <u>that was the opposite of a uniform discriminatory practice.</u> The Court did not believe managers throughout the company would all exercise their discretion in a common way – against women. Simply put, there was "no convincing proof of a companywide discriminatory pay and promotion policy."

Wal-Mart stated that the Court made the right decision and reiterated that it has had strong policies against discrimination for many years.

In fact, <u>a post on Wal-Mart's corporate Web site by Vice President Gisel Ruiz during oral argument stated:</u> "We were pleased to be able to show the Court that Wal-Mart had a strong non-discrimination policy in place well before the lawsuit was filed, and to illustrate the other flaws in Betty Dukes and the others theories."

According to the Court's opinion, this corporate policy was sufficient for it to conclude that the only commonality was that Wal-Mart had a policy of giving local supervisors discretion over employment matters.

On a different but related issue, the Court also rejected Betty dukes and the others claims for back pay and held they too may not be certified. (*Provide a safe and reliable way to easily identify as being authentic.*)

In the separate opinion, Justice Ruth Bader Ginsburg criticized the majority's analysis. While she generally agreed that Betty Dukes and the others claims should not have been certified for procedural reasons under Rule 23(b)(2)- (The court also permitted a large aggregated monetary claim to be certified under the arguably more lenient Rule 23(b)(2), and it reserved for later consideration issues that potentially go to the heart of whether a class-wide trial actually could be conducted fairly.)

She argued they may be certifiable under Rules 23(b)(3)- (Common "questions of law or fact" predominate over any individual questions, and that a class action is the superior method to make a formal judgment or decision.

The district court found that the predominance requirement was satisfied because <u>liability would turn on a single "set of operative facts</u> .... Betty Dukes and the others were either exposed to sexual discrimination or they were not." While recognizing that class members might present a wide variety of damages issues, the court determined that the "common liability issues can be tried in a single class action trial with any individual issues of damages reserved for individual treatment.")

If Betty Dukes and the others could demonstrate common class questions "predominate" over issues affecting individuals. In fact, Justice Ginsburg recognized, "The risk of discrimination is heightened when those managers are pre-dominantly of one sex, and are steeped in a corporate culture that perpetuates gender stereotypes," and that "discretionary employment practices" may spawn discriminatory results, particularly when an employer has vague criteria for evaluating candidates in place.

Citing [*Watson v. Fort Worth Bank & Trust], Justice Ginsberg continued: "A system of delegated discretion, [*Watson] held, is a practice actionable under Title VII when it produces discriminatory outcomes."

For employers, this case will no doubt be cited in a variety of class action proceedings nationwide for the proposition that without common injury and common answers as to why certain conduct took place, class treatment of employee claims is improper.

The Supreme Court voted 5 to 4 in favor of Wal-Mart and did not bring the case for a vote.

Why bring up this issue? Employers may look at the results and determine that the court approves discrimination and justifies lower pay and less spendable money- thereby lowering the standard of living for all employees. The most damaging issue is trying to establish future class actions unless complete information is obtained by all those bring action.

The Next Topic will discuss moving into a third world country. The poverty level is increasing and the middle classes earning have been stagnant over the last 30 years. The banking scandals, the mortgage bubbles have broken, fraud, and outsourcing robbed manufacturing jobs in this country.

Chapter 15 -Moving into a Third World Country

Unemployment

One of the highest unemployment cities in the United States is Las Vegas where the housing market, security market, and banking scandals caused business closures and unemployment now close to 30%. Banks are not lending money to small business because they are not sure if they will still be in business. Lack of money circulation puts the entire economy, not only in Las Vegas, but the entire country into a downward spiral toward a depression.

The United States has reached a vast difference between the very rich, middle class and poor, where the rich are getting richer, and the middle class and poor's money creation is stagnant, and reaching proportions as large as the great depression in the 1930's.

From Wikipedia, the free encyclopedia- The government's definition of poverty is not tied to an absolute value of how much an individual or family can afford, but is tied to a *relative level* based on total income received. For example, the poverty level for 2011 was set at $22,350 (total yearly income) for a family of four. Most Americans (58.5%) will spend at least one year below the poverty line at some point between ages 25 and 75. There remains some controversy over whether the official poverty threshold over- or understates poverty.

Changes are needed to restore the middle class and those in poverty and raise everyone to a better lifestyle.

What good is the U.S. treasury if they do not have the capability to print money to be used to lower the poverty level?

Ideas on Job Creation-

On May 15, 2011 the History channel program "Inspector America" took place in Las Vegas where the city has grown very large over the years. The inspector was examining Lake Mead where the water level had fallen over 140 feet within the last <u>ten years.</u>

The inspector stated that some areas around the United States lack water and other places have floods and that water should be moved where floods constantly occur to those cities and areas that need water. Flood waters around Las Vegas are now being channeled and moved into Lake Mead. This is a great idea, however rainfall in Las Vegas is limited and may not relieve the problems.

The inspector stated that Las Vegas gets electrical power from the Hoover Dam that created Lake Mead, and stated if the <u>water level falls an additional 40 feet the turbines that produce electrical power for Las Vegas would stop.</u> Projects of moving water, building alternative energy projects, and many <u>new ideas should have started when the city started to expand.</u>

Lack of funds by states, cities and municipalities started budget problems that could lead to disaster. The current budget systems used by the government, states, cities and municipalities need revising to keep debt problems from occurring and to do the common good with money provided by the government. Evaluating what is new around the world that may be useful requires research. Why do research from other countries? If you are planning to fix or recreate something and there are competing products, why reinvent something new if the product is in existence and already proven.

Research Other Places for Ideas-

The first step is to start doing research for ideas that will broaden your mind toward new happenings around the world. The idea is to keep you current on reading and discussing ideas from many sources.

If you only read one newspaper, or watch the news on the same TV channel all the time, or discuss topics from <u>one source</u> you never can broaden your knowledge and have discussions on opposing ideas. The same applies in business where competition and new ideas come from all sources around the world. One of the sources to stay current on technology and medical information is from the web site *israel21c.org.*

This site offers tabs with different information and also has a *search field* that would give you related information from past historical reports.

Quite some time ago in reviewing the technology site about an article on <u>biofuel research</u> was a question of what did they use to grease the wheels on carts in ancient times? They didn't use olive oil because of the cost, but they found that the <u>caster bean</u> plant grew wild and didn't require a lot of water and could grow on poor soil.

After <u>three years</u> of evaluating and testing they found a variety of the bean that could produce <u>50% oil</u>. Once that was discovered they were able to find companies that were able to join them. They made a deal to grow the plants in Africa that offered large land masses needed to produce the crops for future harvesting and the production of fuel.

A week later in reviewing an article in a newspaper a company in the United States was looking at stinkweed as a source for biofuel. They were going to spend three years to determine if the plants were a viable source.

In corresponding by e-mail to the owner of that company I attached a copy of the article about the caster bean tests and findings and asked him the following question. "Why do you want to reinvent the wheel when there is an Israeli company that found what you are looking for?" In his e-mail response he thanked me for the article and within a weeks' time his company made a deal with the Israeli company.

Lack of research on evaluating what has been done before is critically needed here in the United States to speed up and move us forward into the 21st century.

In doing more research in israel21c.org using the search field under the technology tab you will discover an article called "pulling out the pistons for 100 miles to the gallon." Under the medical tab using the search field there is an article called "closing in on cancer." It absolutely blows one's mind when reading these articles, as they are nowhere else to be found.

You should look at the accomplishments available today. In reviewing a follow-up on the turbine engine by looking at the <u>Agam Energy Company</u> web site and then sending out an e-mail asking questions about <u>18 wheeler trucks getting *6* miles to the gallon here in the united states, they came back with an answer of getting *18* miles to the gallon.</u> The company goal is to produce electrical power of about 40 megawatt by 2011 and to produce the car engine for Israel by 2012.

Why not pay a royalty for building the cars and engines here in the United States? That would put a lot of people to work and also relieve the gasoline and oil problems. That would be something to think about. *Actually if a car used their engine and batteries, what kind of mileage would you expect?* In my latest correspondence they stated that the engine was evaluated by GE for about 1 ½ years and GE purchased the engine for an electrical power source.

Can you imagine companies here in the United States having the capability of developing this engine for cars, trucks, tractors, boats, combine, etc.? Look at the jobs created here.

A Challenge- Have you looked around your neighborhood and found something that needs fixing or replaced? Check with your neighbors and see what they say. How long do you have to wait for something to happen?

This is referring to all the roads and highways around the united States being repaired, old antiquated sewer systems that need upgrading, bridges that need fixing, overgrown weeds, dilapidated buildings, poverty areas that need upgrading, trash that should be picked up, areas that should be planted and beautified, flooding, fires, control of pollution caused by businesses or neglect, corrosion or decomposition, and the list goes on and on. We know these projects are needed and it is absolutely ridiculous not to have money to do these projects.

Are you tired of being complacent and want this country to stop moving toward a third world country? Too long, many of us and a lot of members of congress, state, and local officials have been a *Me* Society-- instead of a *We* Society. Everyone should start reacting to get this society working and building a *We* Society.

Why do we have to put up with things that need changes and wait for disasters to occur before action is taken? So how do we start? The *We Society* looks at ideas for the common good. Some may think this is Socialism. It definitely is not.

Definition of Socialism-

1: any of various economic and political theories advocating collective or governmental ownership and administration of the means of production and distribution of goods. 2 *a* : a system of <u>society</u> or group living in which there is no private property *b* : a system or condition of society in which the means of production are owned and controlled by the state. 3: a stage of society in <u>Marxist</u> theory transitional between <u>capitalism</u> and <u>communism</u> and distinguished by unequal distribution of goods and pay according to work done.

Definition of Society-

1: companionship or association with one's fellows. 2: a voluntary association of individuals for common ends; *especially*: an organized group working together or periodically meeting because of common interests, beliefs, or profession. 3 *a* : an enduring and cooperating social group whose members have developed organized patterns of relationships through interaction with one another *b* : a community, nation, or broad grouping of people having common traditions, institutions, and collective activities and interests. 4 *a* : a part of a community that is a unit distinguishable by particular aims or standards of living or conduct : a social circle or a group of social circles having a clearly marked identity

Now that you understand about Socialism and society- move your ideas to becoming a *We* Society and fix what needs fixing.

The Next Topic will discuss just a few ideas. Some of these ideas are education, health care, moving out of poverty, treating everyone as you would like to be treated.

Just a Few Ideas

The first thing we should think about is health care for all. That includes dental. OK, if you like your health care companies keep it. Increase medical research and follow up on new ideas.

Jobs can be created by fixing the problems you mentioned for you, your neighbors, and friends.

Education is necessary- we need great schools, dedicated teachers, parents helping kids to learn, sports, music, nurses, good quality food for lunch, tutoring, for colleges- financial aid, math, sciences, money managing and job training.

How about moving people out of poverty- Building new housing- education- jobs- etc.?

For workers- union options, collective bargaining, good salaries, retirement options, decent working conditions and if a person leaves- being able to take their retirement options to the new job.

Those that are under the thumb in working for corporations or special interest groups accepting favors of money or other types of compensation-- should divulge who gives them, whatever they get- and should either leave office or give everything back. If they insist on keeping their compensation, favors or money, they

should excuse themselves from voting whenever any issue comes up by the people or companies they represent.
This is a brief write-up on things that need fixing and it cannot be accomplished unless we understand we need to change the current monetary and budgeting system by the government, states, cities, municipalities, etc.

Chapter 16- Some Final Thoughts

As far back in history as you can remember, those that controlled the money controlled everything.

The Pharaohs in Egypt had the money and power to do anything they wanted. Who was going to oppose them? All those with less status paid, tax or whatever you want to call it, to keep them in power. If they had someone that wanted to oppose them, warfare, or whatever, they appointed others to die for them and their country. You never heard of them actually doing the fighting. They always pointed their finger stating "you do the fighting and dying for me." Their lifestyle was fabulous and those that did things for them lived in poverty.

The kings, queens, dukes, and "royal families" collected taxes to keep their empire going. They never paid for anything. If you look at the royal family in England today, they live on a salary paid by everyone in England. How would you like a lifestyle like that where you get everything you ever wanted and didn't have to worry where the money came from?

We have major corporations in all types of industries, bankers, insurance companies; the security market and anyone dealing with supplying the armed services with equipment and services, get money and are not eager to stop the flow. They don't pay tax and use those in congress to change laws in their favor.

So the question is what changes occurred over multiple generations to create the Pharaohs, "royal families," and all those mentioned above.

Let's start with deception, greed, corruption, murder, you name it. In the 20th century you had the Mafia control Las Vegas, bank robbers, illicit drug sales, alcohol sales during prohibition, and swindlers in all types of industries, corruption in politics, everything to make a "buck." Nothing has changed since then with the exception of using more advanced ideas to pick everyone's pocket without even knowing what's happening.

All of a sudden something happens that creates a striving to make changes hopefully for the better. Of course those in control don't want to lose, so they strike back. This sounds like the change of governments in Egypt and other countries and the fighting in Libya and Syria.

People finally started to figure out they have been duped for years and are looking for change. Now changes are in process with revolts against those causing the problems by fighting and dying for a complete change.

Lincoln did make changes because the bankers were thieves and there was a need to create treasury money to maintain society as the Union desired and he paid a price. Kennedy wanted to get away from the

Federal Reserve and use the money to pay off the debt and he also paid a price.

A Thought to President Obama-

Today we are starting to understand our banking and monetary system, and we are shocked, dismayed, and furious at what we are discovering. The wizard behind the curtain turns out to be a small group of men pulling levers and dials, creating an illusory money scheme that, behind all the talk and bravado, is mere smoke and mirrors.

These levers are controlled by a privately-owned, unaccountable central bank called the Federal Reserve, which has recently dispensed billions if not trillions in funds to its banker cronies, without revealing where these monies are going even under Congressional inquiry or in response to Freedom of Information Act (FOIA) requests. As Chris Powell pointed out recently in conjunction with an FOIA request brought by Bloomberg News, which the Fed declined to comply with:

"Any government that can disburse trillions secretly, without any accountability, is not a democratic government. It is government of, by, and, for the bankers." There was a time when private central bankers were the heavyweights in control, able to run their ultra-secret agenda with impunity; but that era is coming to an end. The bankers are scrambling, trying to patch up their crumbling creations with schemes, bailouts and sleight of hand. That effort, however, must ultimately prove futile. As investment adviser Rolfe Winkler said in a recent article: "The great Ponzi scheme that is the Western

World's economy has grown so big there's simply no 'fixing' it. Flushing more debt through the system would be like giving Madoff a few billion to tide him over. The collapse is already here.

The bankers are on the run, feverishly trying to use the collapse of the current system to steer us toward a North American currency, or a one-world private banking system and privately-issued global currency that they and only they control.

We will not accept those solutions, however, no matter how bad things get. We demand real solutions that empower us, not further enslave us. <u>Abraham Lincoln</u> had such a solution. President <u>Obama</u>, you can finally bring his monetary solution to fruition.

Manifest the vision of Lincoln, Jefferson, Madison and Franklin, and we will make sure you are placed in the pantheon of our greatest leaders and are revered for all time. America's greatest days can still be ahead of us; but for this to happen, *we need to expose and root out the deceptive banking scheme that would enslave us to a future of debt and increasing homelessness in this great country our forefathers founded.* The time has come for democracy to become superior to a private banking cartel and take back the power to create money once again. Such a transformation would represent the most epochal and empowering shift that humanity has ever seen. As you recently said:

"This country has never responded to a crisis by sitting on the sidelines and hoping for the best. Throughout our history we have met every great challenge with bold action and big ideas."

Your words are a timely reminder of our long legacy of action and bold solutions in the face of adversity. Can we do this? Yes we can.

The ideas I am proposing are different.

I just want to have the states have banks to lower the risks and work with the Federal Reserve, but have restrictions against them. Other state banks for the common good could be established where money comes directly from the *treasury* used strictly for the common good. You named what needs fixing and changes that have to be made. *The question is- <u>are we going to start "revolting" to get the changes for the common good?</u>*

Now that you read about what needs to be done to fix the economy, we have to answer what has to be done to move us or our business into a more profitable position? The changes will hopefully be done in our lifetime.

The biggest changes affecting everyone- is the outsourcing starting from the end of the Second World War. I presented ideas on being proactive, looking at your resume in a different light, telling why businesses fail, protecting and tracking your savings, and ideas from CPA's, thinking outside the box, on the idea of the inflation saving health plan, and others. You may come up with your own ideas, but to be successful today, move your thoughts to the *We* Society Ideas, and away from the *Me* Society. Money is necessary, but relationships with your clients and others are "The Keys to Success."